Landscapes of
CORSICA
a countryside guide
Second edition

KU-330-829

Noel Rochford

SUNFLOWER
BOOKS

For Chris

Revised printing 1994
Second edition 1993
Sunflower Books
12 Kendrick Mews
London SW7 3HG, UK

© copyright 1993, 1994
Sunflower Books.
All rights reserved. No part of this
publication may be reproduced,
stored in a retrieval system, or
transmitted by any form or by any means,
electronic, mechanical,
photocopying, recording or
otherwise, without the prior written
permission of the publishers.

ISBN 1-85691-012-1

Corsican pine

Important note to the reader

I have tried to ensure that the descriptions and maps in this book are error-free at press date. The book will be updated, where necessary, whenever future printings permit. It will be very helpful for us to receive your comments (send them to the publishers, please) for the updating of future printings.

I also rely on those who use this book — especially walkers — to take along a good supply of common sense when they explore. Conditions change fairly rapidly on Corsica, and *storms, fires or bulldozing may make a route unsafe at any time.* If the route is not as I outline it here, and your way ahead is not secure, return to the point of departure. *Never attempt to complete a tour or walk under hazardous conditions!* Please read carefully the notes on pages 52 to 57, the country code on page 136, and the introductory comments at the beginning of each tour and walk (regarding road conditions, equipment, grade, distances and time, etc). Explore *safely*, while at the same time respecting the beauty of the countryside.

Special note: Corsica is prone to summer forest fires. Please do not light fires; do all you can to keep the island green and beautiful.

Cover photograph: Monte Renoso
Photographs: Noel Rochford and John Underwood
Touring map: John Theasby and Pat Underwood
Walking maps adapted from the IGN Série Orange 1:50,000 (Corsica; Numbers 4149-53, 4250-4, 4256, 4348), reproduced by permission of the Institut Géographique Nationale
Drawings: Sharon Rochford
Printed and bound in the UK by The Devonshire Press Ltd, Torquay

Contents

Silver birch

Olive

Plane

.Beech

Chestnut

Holm oak

Kermes oak

Olive

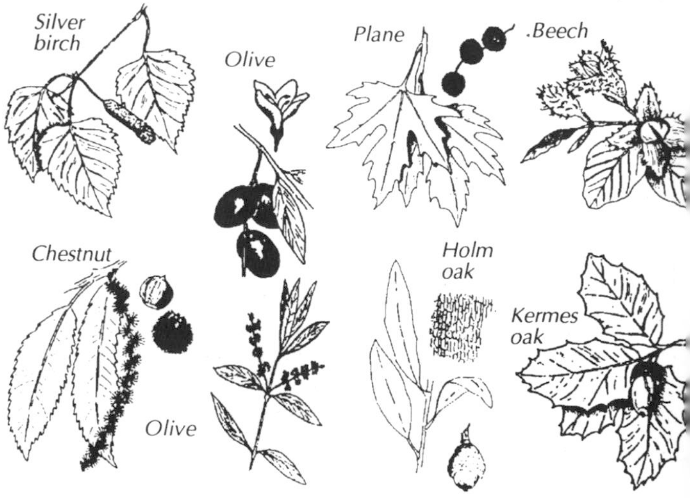

❋ Preface

Corsica is often referred to as the 'Isle of Beauty', or the 'Scented Isle'; both are very fitting, but I'd like to propose another name: the 'Friendly Isle'. The constant friendliness of the Corsicans towards me outshone all else. Unlike most tourist resorts, it was the rule rather than the exception. Renting an apartment was more like staying with friends than a business affair, and asking for directions ended up in friendly chats, before being lead to my path. And perhaps most extraordinary of all: friendly and helpful tourist offices (*syndicats d'initiative*)! A rarity in the world of tourism. Corsica, I discovered, is unique!

No other Mediterranean island can boast such a wealth of natural beauty. Beaches to suit every taste: from long stretches of glaring white sand to pink rocky coves. *Real* mountains — climbers' terrain — that reach almost 3000m/9000ft. In these mountains you stumble upon a magnificent mixture of pine forests, beech woods, chestnut groves, and coppices of evergreen oaks. Streams bound down the mountainsides; rivers cascade through awe-inspiring gorges, leaving behind blue-green pools as clear as crystal. The pink granite hills and cliffs, normally conjured up only for an artist's canvas, are real indeed on Corsica.

In spring the countryside is enlivened with a tapestry of wild flowers and maquis in bloom. The hills are ablaze with colour; the air is intoxicatingly scented by the maquis.

For history buffs, the island is littered with evidence of its turbulent past, dating from about 6000BC. Rudimentary megalithic monuments still lie where they were placed thousands of years ago — in fields and out in the maquis-clad hills. The severe and simple Romanesque churches draw you to a halt with the precision of their masonry. Enchanting, story-book villages, many dating from the Middle Ages, adorn the landscape. They perch atop rocky spurs, or high on mountainsides, enjoying 'belvedere' views. And one cannot forget to mention the name of Napoleon who, it seems, did little for his native Corsica. Nevertheless, the Corsicans are proud of this part of their heritage.

The sheer unspoilt beauty of Corsica is enough to turn anyone into an explorer, be it on foot or by car. Driving around, you get itchy feet just looking at the never-ending beauty spots. You may not be a walker, but you'll soon find yourself wandering off into the countryside. The splendidly-located picnic spots will lure you from your vehicle into the magnetic landscape. Nowhere will you get more pleasure out of walking, whether you choose a short stroll or you tackle the GR20. Driving is equally enjoyable. Corsica is still far from flooded with tourists, as your tours in the countryside will prove. Crossing vast uninhabited tracts of land, you often pass more livestock than vehicles.

Corsica cannot guarantee you the eternal sunshine of, say, the Canaries — or even the prolonged summer of most of the Mediterranean islands. So if it's swimming and sunning you're after, visit Corsica in high season. But if walking is your priority, go in spring for the flowers or in autumn when the trees are turning colour and the shepherds are returning to the valleys with their flocks.

I hope that, armed with *Landscapes of Corsica,* you will discover the real island, and its friendly face.

Acknowledgements

Very special thanks to the following people for their help and encouragement:
Geoff Daniel, for encouraging me to write this book;
Pauline Hallam, French Tourist Office, London;
L'Agence Régionale du Tourisme et des Loisirs, Ajaccio;
Mlle Torre, Parc Naturel Régional de la Corse;
L'Office National des Forêts (Ajaccio and Bastia);
Marianne Chodjai, Office Municipal du Tourisme, Calvi;
Françoise McCullin, Syndicat d'Initiative, Calvi (and M Noël);
Mme Casanova, Syndicate d'Initiative, Bastia;
M et Mme Prédali, and the Flore Gino family, for their kindness;
My family, friends and publisher, for their support;
My sister, Sharon, for her lovely drawings;
The staff at the Hotel Belvedere, Ajaccio.

Recommended books and maps

Roland Grant, *Blue Guide Corsica* (A & C Black, 1992)
Corse (Michelin, in French only);
Le Guide Corse de la Corse (tourist booklet available on the island, from local *syndicats d'initiative* (in French only);
Parc Naturel Régional de la Corse guides to the island's flora, etc (available on Corsica, in French);
For touring: Michelin map No 90 (*Corse*); scale 1:200,000;
For walking: IGN 'Série Orange' maps (as reproduced in this book; scale 1:50,000; 22 sheets!). Also: the Didier-Richard 2-sheet map (*Itinéraires pédestres*); scale 1:50,000 covers many walking routes.

✸ Getting about

Corsica is a large island indeed, and the public transport network is limited, especially outside high season. The problem is best solved by hiring a vehicle for either part or all of your vacation. Some package holidays have very good **fly/drive** arrangements, so do investigate these ... if it's not too late.

The SNCF runs a good **train** service connecting Ajaccio, Corte, l'Ile-Rousse, Calvi, and Bastia. This is an excellent way to see the interior of the island and reach the mountain walks.

Local **buses** are always fun, but are few and far between. Tourists will find them mostly unsuitable, since scheduling serves the needs of the local community (eg, mail or school buses). In the high season (July to September), however, there are some special 'tourist route' buses which are more helpful for getting about — although not necessarily for getting to and from walks.

Taxis are another way of getting around Corsica. They are very expensive, however, and only economical when shared by a few people. Agree on a price before setting out, and don't be afraid to bargain.

Coach tours may appeal to some of you: you will get to see the major tourist sights and routes in comfort, with the minimum effort.

The **town plans** on the following three pages show you where to board your bus or train in Ajaccio, Calvi, or Bastia. These plans also show exits for motorists; they are keyed to the main roads shown on the touring map.

Timetables for the buses and trains used for the walks in this book are found on pages 129-133; due to space limitations, we have been unable to include timetables for *all* public transport operating on the island. Remember, too, that no timetable in a book can ever be as up-to-date as one you can obtain from the local tourist offices (bus timetables) or the SNCF railway station nearest your base. So when you arrive on Corsica, *do* call in at the railway and tourist offices, where you can arm yourself not only with timetables, but with all manner of helpful reading material.

One of the nicest things about getting around Corsia is the availability of good maps!

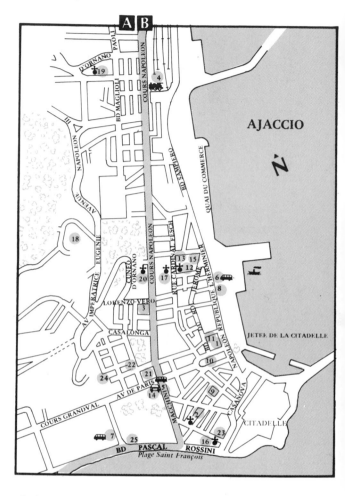

AJACCIO

 1 Tourist information
 2 Cathedral
 3 PTT (post, telephones)
 4 Trains
 5 Buses
 6 Buses (gare routière)
 7 Buses to La Parata
 8 Boats, ferries
 9 Maison Bonaparte
10 Place Maréchal Foch
11 Musée Napoléonien
12 Chapelle Impériale

13 Musée Fesch (art museum)
14 Place Général-de-Gaulle
15 Palais Fesch (library)
16 Eglise St-Erasme
17 Petit St-Roch
18 Hospital
19 St-Antoine
20 St-Roch
21 Police headquarters
22 Parks Information Centre
23 Musée du Capitellu
24 Musée Bandero
25 Casino

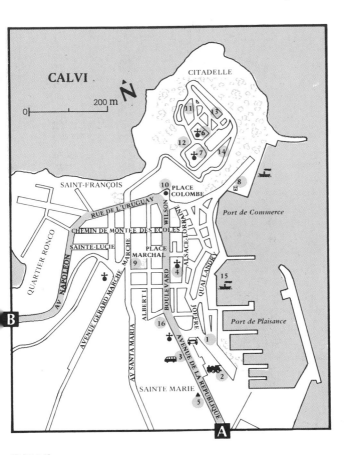

CALVI

1 Tourist information
2 Trains
3 Buses
4 Eglise St-Marie-Majeure
5 Youth hostel
6 Eglise St-Jean-Baptiste
7 Oratoire de la Confrérie
  St-Antoine
8 Tour du Sel
9 Town hall/police
10 Place Christophe Colomb

11 'Birthplace' of Christopher
   Columbus
12 Caserne Sampiero (old
   palace of the Genoese
   governors)
13 Maison Pacciola (where
   Napoleon stayed)
14 Palais Giubega
15 Boats (Girolata, etc)
16 PTT (post, telephones)

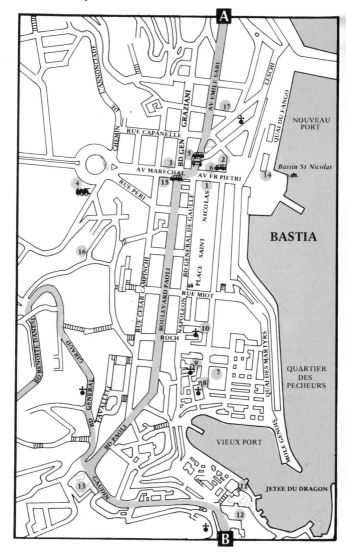

BASTIA

1 Tourist information
2 Town hall
3 PTT (post, telephones)
4 Trains
5 Buses (public transport)
6 Buses ('Cap Corse Tour')
7 Market (Pl. de l'Hôtel de Ville)
8 Eglise St-Jean-Baptiste
9 Immaculate Conception

10 St-Roch
11 Jardin Romieu
12 Museum of Corsican
   Ethnology
13 Law courts
14 Ships, ferries
15 Buses for Porto-Vecchio
16 Clinic
17 Air France

❀ Picnicking

Corsica is unbeatable for picnicking. On the following pages I have listed just a few of my favourite picnic spots (each is described), but there are hundreds upon hundreds of natural, unspoiled locations. There are also some 'official' picnic sites with tables, benches and fountains; those on or near the touring routes have been highlighted in the touring notes and on the touring map with the symbol ⌱.

All the information you need to get to the fourteen picnic spots I particularly recommend is given on the following pages. *Picnic numbers correspond to walk numbers*, so you can quickly find the general location on the island by referring to the touring map (where walks are outlined in white). I give transport details (🚗 = car parking; 🚐 = how to get there by bus), walking times, and views or setting. Beside the picnic title you will find a map reference: the location of the picnic spot is shown on this *walking map*, labelled with the symbol *P*. Several of the picnic places are illustrated.

Most of these picnic spots are reached after a very short, easy walk. In fact, together with the short walk suggestions on page 14, they make *excellent rambles for 'non-walkers'*. Several are along the routes of car tours and ideal for stretching your legs. Do, however, look over the comments before setting out: if some walking is involved, remember to wear sensible shoes. Always take a **sunhat** with you (○ indicates a picnic in **full sun**). Take along a plastic sheet as well, in case the ground is damp or prickly.

Fill your hamper with the exquisite local cheeses (*brocciu* is a good one), *charcutérie* (try *coppa* and *lonza*), fresh fruit, *embrocciata* (a cheese tartlet) and of course wine.

All picnickers should read the country code on page 136 and go quietly in the countryside. *Bon appetit!*

---

1 POINTE DE LA PARATA (map page 58) ○

by car or taxi: 25-35min on foot   *by bus: 25-35min on foot*
🚗 Park at the end of the road to the Pointe de la Parata (D111).
🚐 (town bus) from Ajaccio to the Pointe de la Parata (Timetable 1)
Follow Walk 1 for up to 25min. No shade. In spring this area is like a vast bouquet of flowers. A similar setting is shown on page 59.

11

4 FORÊT DOMANIALE DE CHIAVARI (map page 66)

by car or taxi: 5-10min on foot   *by bus: 15-20min on foot*
🚗 Park on the forestry track off the D55 northeast of Verghia (about 700m before the Coti-Chiavari turn-off); a small rock inscribed 'Forêt Domaniale de Chiavari' lies at the entrance.
🚌 to Verghia (Timetable 6); then follow Walk 4 for 15-20min
Picnic anywhere amidst the cork trees and pines. A highly recommended short walk begins here (1h20min); see 'Short walk', page 67. Note that the striking beach just across the road is also a good spot for picnicking/swimming.

5 CASCADES DES ANGLAIS (map on reverse of touring map)

by car or taxi: 25-35 min on foot   *by bus: 25-35min on foot*
🚗 Park in la Foce, a hamlet just north of Col de Vizzavona on the N193 (the first houses you come to, when you cross the pass from Ajaccio). Or park some 200m/yds below the hamlet on the forestry track entrance on your left, where there is a small sign for the 'cascades'. Don't block the track!
🚌 Corte/Bastia bus from Ajaccio to la Foce (Timetable 7)
Follow Walk 5 to the tumbling river (25min). Picnic here, or follow the walk beside the falls for another 10-15min. You'll find exquisite green pools and smooth rock slopes; this is a splendid mountain scene, set in a beech forest. It is a popular spot during high season and on weekends, but it's easy to lose the crowds. The photograph on page 70 was taken further along the walk, but the setting is similar.

7 MURACCIOLE (map on reverse of touring map)

by car or taxi: 10-20min on foot   *by bus: not easily accessible*
🚗 Park at Muracciole, 2km east of Vivario (D343 south of Corte).
From the church follow the signposts for Vivario and descend into the valley below. Keep right at the fork, beyond which you can choose your picnic spot in beautiful fresh countryside of fields and tree-clad hills. You might be tempted to try the (easy) short walk to Vivario and back (see 'Short walk 2', page 73).

9 PONTE VECCHIU/PONT DE ZAGLIA (map pages 82-83; photograph page 82)

by car or taxi: 5-30min on foot   *by bus: not easily accessible*
🚗 Park near 'les Deux Ponts d'Ota', not far below Ota, on the D124 (or turn off the D84 midway between Porto and Evisa).
Follow the path to the left of the second bridge (when coming from Ota) and head up into the Gorges de Spelunca. You'll come to the Genoese foot-bridge shown on page 82 in 30min. This is a very popular route in high season, with plenty of places to picnic and swim. The Ponte Vecchiu is a little closer to Ota (you can see it from the side of the road). It's also an excellent picnicking/swimming spot.

11 LES CALANCHE (map page 88; photograph page 32) ○

by car or taxi: 10-25min on foot   *by bus: 10-25min on foot*
🚗 Park in the lay-by at 'les Roches Bleues' (bar) on the D81 between Porto and Piana (don't park in the lay-by 'for buses only').
🚌 Ota/Porto bus to les Roches Bleues (Timetable 2)
Follow the D81 uphill for 5min: you'll see a sign on a pine tree in a lay-by, 'Chemin des Muletiers'. After a steep uphill scramble lasting 10min, you overlook the weird and wonderful Calanche. Little shade.

12 NOTRE DAME DE LA SERRA (map page 89; photo page 91) ○

by car or taxi: up to 5min on foot   *by bus: not easily accessible*
🚗 Park at the chapel of Notre Dame de la Serra, signposted off the
D81b, 4km south of Calvi.
*Sit on the balcony and look out over Calvi and the gulf, or climb to
the viewpoint on the hillock on the left side of the chapel (no shade).*

13 SANT' ANTONINO (map pages 92-93; photograph page 95) ○

by car or taxi: 10-15min on foot   *by bus: not easily accessible*
🚗 Park in Sant' Antonino, by the church. Best approached from the
D71 or the D151 south of l'Ile-Rousse: turn off onto the D413
between Aregno and Cateri.
*Picnic in the middle of the village on the hilltop, from where you'll
have a view of Algajola Bay, the inland mountains, and over Sant'
Antonino itself. It's surprisingly quiet here. There is no shade, but a
breeze often blows over the hill. Superb setting for an evening picnic.*

15 BONIFATU (map pages 98-99) 🛆

by car or taxi: up to 5min on foot   *by bus: not easily accessible*
🚗 Park in the car park below the inn at Bonifatu. Travelling south
from Calvi, turn-off the airport road and follow the D251 to its end.
*There is an organised picnic site set in a forest alongside a stream, just
across the bridge beyond the forestry house. To get away from the
crowds, wander up the forestry track alongside the river.*

16 TUVARELLI (map pages 100-101)

by car or taxi: 5-10min on foot   *by bus: not easily accessible*
🚗 Park in Tuvarelli. Turn east off the D81 to follow the D351 up the
Fango Valley: Tuvarelli is the first hamlet you reach. Park at the side
of the road near the Pont de Tuvarelli-Chiorna, or drive down the
track shown on the map and park on the north side of the bridge.
*The river here makes a perfect picnicking spot. You can sit on the
rocky banks and overlook the deep clear pools. If you're really after
solitude, you have the entire valley at your disposal, all 13.5km of it!*

22 BERGERIE DE GROTTELLE (map page 121)

by car or taxi: 10-30min on foot   *by bus: not easily accessible*
🚗 Park in the car parking area at the end of the Restonica Gorge
road (D623). This road branches off the N193 south of Corte.
*There are endless picnicking places all along the D623. However, if
you follow the notes for Walk 22 (page 120), you can find an especially pretty spot on grassy inclines overlooking a stream (when you
come to the fork 25min up, go left to follow the easier path).*

23 BAVELLA (map page 122; photograph page 123)

by car or taxi: up to 25min on foot   *by bus: up to 25min on foot*
🚗 Park in Bavella, on the D268, 9km northeast of Zonza.
🚌 Porto Vecchio/Ajaccio bus to Bavella (Timetable 5; *high season
only*).
*Picnic at the pass itself, near the parking bay (where the photograph
on page 123 was taken). Otherwise follow Walk 23 for 25min, to
where a path forks off left from the track. Here there's a grassy nodule
jutting out off the hillside — a super place to picnic, under pine trees
and with views towards the dramatic rose-coloured valley walls.*

Cyclamen

24 CASCADE DE PISCIA DI GALLO (map page 125; photograph page 124)

by car or taxi: 20-25min on foot
by bus: 20-25min on foot

🚗 Park at the waterfall turn-off, either on the side of the road (D368) or in the parking area of the nearby snack bar ('La Cascada'), 700m north (over the wall) of the Barrage de l'Ospedale.

🚌 as for Picnic 23, to the snack bar La Cascada
The waterfall is only 40 minutes away, but if that's too far, you have a good overview of the surrounding landscape only twenty minutes into Walk 24.

25 BONIFACIO (map page 126; photographs pages 127, 128) ◯

by car or taxi: 10-25min on foot
by bus: 10-25min on foot

🚗 Park in Bonifacio.

🚌 from Porto-Vecchio to Bonifacio (Timetable 19, high season only)

Follow Walk 25 to picnic anywhere along the magnificent limestone cliffs. Admittedly, it's hard to get away from the crowds. The maquis will give you limited privacy, but very little shade. This stretch of coastline is so irresistible that you may be enticed into doing the whole walk.

Short walk suggestions

The suggestions below, together with the 'picnic walks', are particularly suitable for non-walkers and very warm days.

Short walk 1, description p 58, photograph p 59

Walk 3, description p 63: walk as far as you like from the Col St-Georges; return the same way. Or walk along the Plage de Porticcio to the airport (1h15min); see the end of the Alternative walk on p 63 and photograph p 66.

Short walk 4, description p 67

Walk 6, description p 71, photograph p 20: follow the track beyond Canaglia as far as you like.

Short walk 7-2, description p 73

Short walk 11, description p 85, photograph p 87

Alternative walk 12, description p 89: do all or only part of it.

Walk 13, description and photograph p 95: walk from Sant' Antonino to the Capu Corbinu and back.

Short walk 16-1, desription p 101, photo p 103

Short walk 17, description and photograph p 104: follow the track as long as you like.

Short walk 18, description p 106, photo p 108

Walk 20: from Tralonca, walk into the valley; notes begin on p 115; photos p 27, 116. To the hut in the photograph and back allow 30min.

Walk 21, description page 117: follow the start of the walk as far as you like.

Anemone

Aquilegia Bernardii

Juniper

Scottish thistle

❀ Touring

Hiring a vehicle (car, motorbike, moped) is the only way really to see Corsica. It is expensive. Motorbike and moped riders often have to leave an enormous deposit as surety. Insurance is extra *and advisable.* Breakdowns are not uncommon, so check your vehicle thoroughly before setting out, and don't take it if you're not happy with it! Ask to see all the rental and insurance conditions *in English*, and make sure you understand them. Carry the rental firm's telephone number (and a number where they can be reached outside office hours) with you. If you pay by credit card, check the amount you sign for and keep all receipts!

The touring notes are brief: they include little history or information about the towns; all this is freely available from local *syndicats d'initiative* (tourist information offices). Instead, I've concentrated on the 'logistics' of touring: times and distances, road conditions, and seeing parts of Corsica that most tourists miss. Most of all, I emphasise possibilites for **walking** and **picnicking** (the symbol *P* is used to alert you to a picnic spot; see pages 11-14). While some of the picnic and short walk suggestions may not be suitable during a long car tour, you may see a landscape that you would like to explore at leisure another day.

Remember that many **petrol stations** (especially inland) will be **closed on Sundays/holidays** ... even on Saturday afternoons! Take along warm clothing and some food and drink; **be prepared for delays** on mountain roads (where passes may be closed in bad weather and where you must drive very carefully, watching for foraging livestock). **Allow enough time:** the tour time only includes brief stops at viewpoints labelled ◉.

The large touring map is designed to be held out opposite the touring notes and contains all the information you need outside the towns. **The tours** (based on Ajaccio, Calvi, Bastia, and Porto-Vecchio) are **numbered according to importance** (thus, if your time is limited, 'Calvi 1' would be the most highly recommended tour from Calvi). **Symbols** used in the text correspond to those on the touring map; see the touring map for a **key.**

Ajaccio 1: THE PINK CLIFFS OF THE PORTO GULF AND THE SPELUNCA GORGE

Ajaccio • Cargèse • Piana • Porto • Ota • Evisa • Vico • Ajaccio

The roads are generally good, but winding. Inland, short stretches are narrow and bumpy, but there's little traffic. Watch out for foraging animals on the inland roads. No petrol stations between Porto and Vico (48km). In early spring and late autumn some mountain passes may be closed. Reckon on 210km/130mi, about 7h driving; take Exit A from Ajaccio (plan page 8).

On route: *P* (see pages 11-14): 9, 11; Walks 2, 8, 9, 10, 11

This tour is packed with unsurpassed coastal scenery. The pink cliffs of the Golfe de Porto are by no means overrated, nor are the intriguing crags of les Calanche. The great inland valleys, with their chestnut and oak forests, will entice you back another day — perhaps for a picnic, a debauchery of local food and superb scenery.

Leave Ajaccio on the main north route (N193; Exit A), following signs for Cargèse/Calvi. Some 6.5km out, just beyond **Mezzavia**, strike off north for Cargèse on the D81. The towering Rocher des Gozzi, shown on page 60, bulges out of the hills on your right, capturing your attention. Walk 2 would take you to the summit, from where there is one of the finest outlooks in the vicinity. Appietto, the starting point for the walk, is signposted (on your right, but easily missed) at 13km.

Climbing over the squat hills that block out the Golfe de Sagone, you look down onto verdant fields lining a seaward valley. The tiny Golfu di Lava sits at its mouth. Scarlet poppies, violet bugloss, dandelions and indigo vetch turn the roadside into a garden. You cross a saddle, the Bocca San Bastiano, and meet with a striking panorama (⊙☞). First you'll see hills stepping their way inland to the 'master peaks' — glimmering white beacons, perhaps still capped in snow. Then the Sagone Gulf distracts you, with its exquisite generous bays of white sand and turquoise water. Pass through a trickle of tourist hamlets and the vast untouched beach that sits at the mouth of the Liamone River. **Sagone** (38km, ▲▲▲△ ✕☞), the junction for Evisa and Vico, follows. Turn left to keep along the coastal D81: further around the gulf, you look back onto the outstretched arm of the Capo di Feno (Walk 1). Soon you're in **Cargèse** (52km ☗▲▲▲ △✕). The village is stepped up a hillside overlooking

16

a cove. This small resort was founded by Greeks, and Roman Catholic and Greek Orthodox churches face each other in the centre; the latter contains some 17th-century icons. Short walk 8 sets out from Cargèse.

Your entry into **Piana** (72km ▲▲▲✕🏠) could not be more grand: coming down from the hills, you look straight across the majestic **Porto Gulf★** (photograph page 86), perhaps the most beautiful in the whole of Europe. This natural harbour of pink granite cliffs rising out of an intensely blue sea is spellbinding. Small green coves sit back in the cliffs. And Piana, perched high above the sea, soaks up this unparalleled panorama. Let's do some exploring. On coming into the village pass the first hotel. Then fork off left on a rough lane for the **Saliccio Belvedere★** (📷). From this viewing point you look out onto the mountainous interior and over the weird rock formations of les Calanche. Hidden in the sheer cliffs below is the tiny cove of Ficajola and, if you drive down to it, you will have a splendid view into the Calanche: return to the D81 and turn off left just before the church (signposted 'Plage d'Arone'). A kilometre along, take the first turning right and zigzag down to **Ficajola★**, from where a path drops you down into this memorable cove. Prefer beach swimming? Return to the turn-off and continue some 10km further, to the Plage d'Arone (91km). An exhilarating drive carries you past **Capu Rossu★**, a mountain of rock hanging off the southern arm of the gulf, adorned by a Genoese watch-tower. When the road forks near the beach, keep left.

From the Plage d'Arone, return to Piana and continue north on the D81. Cross the Pont de Mezanu (where Walk 11 begins) and pass the Chalet des Roches Bleues (*P*11). You're now winding through the pink

Car tour Calvi 3: Pigna is a handicraft centre, with grand buildings and narrow alleys.

The 12th-century chapel of St-Michel, near Murato, boasts some fine sculptures. It's on the route of the optional detour in Car tour Basia 2.

world of **les Calanche★** (; photograph page 32). Guy de Maupassant described it as a 'forest of purple granite'. Walk 11 explores les Calanche in depth. Why not try the short, easy version to the Château Fort? See notes page 85 and photograph page 87.

Out of this 'jungle' of rock, you pass pine-shaded picnic spots (no facilities except rubbish baskets). The gulf reappears, and Porto comes into view. It sits in a poster-like setting ★, best appreciated from above: the rich colour contrasts of the pale-grey pebble beach, blue sea, green vegetation and rose-coloured rock shoreline are a rare sight. **Porto** (114km ◫ ▲▲▲✕🛒🛖), built solely for tourism, is overlooked by a square Genoese watchtower. Continuing past the village, turn inland, swinging sharply back to the right on the D124 towards Ota. Ascending into the deep Porto Valley, you come into olive trees. Spring-green chestnut groves stand out in the dark cloak of the surrounding vegetation.

Ota (119km ▲▲▲✕🛖) is an impressive sight. The village, shown on page 84, is perched high on the hillside amidst olive trees. Pink craggy walls tower overhead. Bump your way down to the **Ponte Vecchiu★** (🛖), the beautifully-restored Genoese foot-bridge seen ahead. This is a perfect picnic spot (**P**9), where you can take an invigorating swim. Expect company, however: it's mentioned in all the guide books. A minute later you cross 'les Deux Ponts d'Ota', two enchanting stone bridges at the confluence of the Onca River and the **Gorges de Spelunca★**. A path cutting off left, immediately beyond the second bridge, would take you up the gorge to

Vineyards on the N196 north of Bonifacio create a scene worthy of an Impressionist master.

the lovely Genoese Pont de Zaglia (photograph page 82; *P*9), another superb picnic spot. Just a few minutes in this glorious countryside will lure you back to complete Walk 9 another day.

From here we climb to a junction and turn sharp left on the D84 for Evisa. The road swings back into another gorge, lush with chestnut groves. Pass two turn-offs for Marignana, where Walk 8 starts. Approaching **Evisa** (137km ▲▲▲△✖), come to a roadside balcony (☎) which gives you a last opportunity to capture all this beauty with a photograph. Walk 9 begins here.

Bear sharp right at the junction outside Evisa to join the D70. From the **Col de Sevi** (1101m/3610ft ☎), you enjoy a fine view back over the Tavulella Valley. On the descent, an immense valley (the Gorges de Liamone) opens up on your left, dominated by the Punta di a Spusata. Turn left into **Vico** (159km ▲▲△✖🛒). A few hundred metres from the junction, bear right for the Couvent de St-François (✝). A wood-carving of Christ in the 15th-century church is claimed to be the oldest on Corsica. Vico is a village full of character, with tall granite buildings lining its alleys and single main street.

To complete the circuit, continue on the D70 to Sagone. You drop down through wooded hills to the Sagone Valley floor. Lush pastures fill the river flat. Alders trickle along the stream banks. In May the fields are flooded with deep blue *Echium* — a dazzling sight. Once in Sagone, head left for Ajaccio on the D81.

Ajaccio 2: COUNTRY ROADS TO BASTELICA

Ajaccio • Porticcio • Coti-Chiavari • Bastelica • Tolla • Ajaccio

The roads are variable, generally narrow and winding. The stretches between Marato and the Col St-Georges and Bastelica and Tolla are exceptionally narrow; some people will find them vertiginous. Be alert for foraging animals on inland roads. No petrol stations between Porticcio and Bastelicaccia (117km). Reckon on 174km/108mi, 7h driving; take Exit B from Ajaccio (plan page 8).

On route: **P** (see pages 11-14): 1, 4 , ⊼ outside Cauro; Walks 1, 3, 4

G et out into the countryside and savour rural Corsica, an island where much of the land remains untamed, covered in maquis and a wealth of forests. In springtime you will be overwhelmed by the extravaganza of wild flowers illuminating the hills. The highlight of this tour is the jade-green Tolla Reservoir. But don't be too late returning to Ajaccio for the fire of pink sunset over the Iles Sanguinaires!

Follow the N196 (main south road, Exit B) out to the Porticcio intersection (11.5km) and turn off on the D55 to **Porticcio** (17.5km ▲▲▲▲△✕☖WC), one of Corsica's largest tourist centres. Its beautiful golden beach and picturesque setting are now the casualties of development. Much of this side of the gulf is 'ritzy-residential'. Following the coast, you curve in and out of pretty bays and coves. Your view extends across the harbour to Ajaccio and the hills behind it.

Approaching Verghia (▲▲△ ✕), you skirt the most beautiful beach on this stretch of coast. The long white sand collar curves round

This splendid waterfall, on the route of Walk 6 to the 'fairytale' Tolla bergerie, may be visited as a detour during Car tour Bastia 2.

This 100m/330ft-high railway bridge, one of Gustave Eiffel's lesser-known works, spans the Vecchio River north of Vivario. Travelling by train into the interior is simply spectacular.

towards a stand of pines. If you would like to see a beautiful wood of cork trees (or, in spring, a deluge of wild flowers) try the short version of Walk 4 and go up into the Forêt Domaniale de Chiavari. The track to it is not well signposted but, as you approach the stand of pines at the end of the beach, keep a look-out for a wide earthen track off left into the cork trees and pines. The lovely picnic area (**P**4) on the edge of the wood is almost in ruins. The main tour continues on the D55, which turns off left less than a kilometre further on (29km) and climbs through a magnificent evergreen forest to **Coti-Chiavari** (39km ▲✕🕋). This small terraced village sits at the foot of a maquis wood, with a fine outlook over the tail of the gulf to the Iles Sanguinaires. Descending from the settlement, you look down onto another tower-crowned headland, the Capu di Muru. Just over 5km beyond Coti-Chiavari, pass the turn-off for the Capu di Muru and bear left.

Splendid coastal views follow you all the way, as you head east over the hills. In the distance ridges pour down off the island's central spine. Below lies the deeply-indented Baie de Cupabia, with an irresistible, untouched beach. If you're ready for a break, this bay may be just what you're looking for: if so, at the next junction bear right for Serra-di-Ferro. A detour of just over 2.5km carries you to the turn-off down to the beach (a rough, winding track not recommended after wet weather). The main tour continues straight on (left) to the next junction: bear left again, on the D355.

You climb into the hills, where goats roam wild. Meet the D55 again, and bear right. Not far beyond **Marato**, the only village out here in 'the wilds', be sure to take the second right-hand turn to continue on the D55 (signposted for Sta-Maria-Siché). Hugging steep rocky hillsides on an exceptionally narrow road lined with dazzling yellow *Coronilla,* you look out over a wooded valley. Keep left all the way to the N196, and there bear left. Climb to the **Col St-Georges** (84km

▲✗🕾). Walk 3, an easy but fairly long ramble, begins just outside the inn here; why not stretch your legs?

Descend from the pass (🍴) and come to the outskirts of Cauro (▲▲✗). Bear sharp right on the D27 before entering the village. You meander along a lush valley occupied by small farms and boskets. Soon you disappear into the high hills again and, 4km before you reach Bastelica, you pass by the turn-off left to Tolla (your return route). Perhaps what you'll remember most about **Bastelica** (109.5km ▲▲▲✗) is the magnificent chestnut wood that surrounds it. Your approach to the village takes you past tired old stone walls that enclose plots and orchards. Some fine old stone mansions are found in the six hamlets that comprise Bastelica, stretching out across the valley inclines. Drive between the houses, keeping straight on at the church, then swing back left beyond the church to return to the Tolla turn-off. Monte Renoso (Corsica's fourth highest peak; 2352m/7715ft; see cover) sits high in the valley.

Your homeward route follows the scenic **Prunelli Gorge★**, a continuation of Bastelica's picturesque valley. Turn right when you reach the Tolla road (D3), a *very* narrow route cut into the gorge walls. Drive *very carefully* and only admire the views where you can pull over off the road *safely*. The river flows far below. Rounding a corner, the gorge opens up, and the jade-green **Lac de Tolla★** (a reservoir) fills the valley floor. What a view! A collar of pink rock, marking the waterline, separates the sherwood green of the wooded hillsides fom the jade-green of the lake. **Tolla** (115.5km ✗🕾) is the village set high on the grassy slopes, overlooking both the dam and the rugged interior. Beyond the village, a lay-by enables you to pull off the road and enjoy the setting (🕾). Crossing the **Bocca di Mercujo** (✗), park at the restaurant and follow the track to the belvedere★ (🕾 10min downhill) for a more spectacular view of the dam and gorge.

Follow the D3 back to the N196 just beyond Bastelicaccia and bear right for Ajaccio. To see the magnificent sunset over the Iles Sanguinaires, go straight through town and follow the coast out to the **Pointe de la Parata**, 12km west (✗🕾*P*1, Walk 1). Find yourself a soft piece of ground and let it all take place...

Ajaccio 3: SOME HISTORY ... AND THE D69

Ajaccio • Col St-Georges • Filitosa • Propriano • Campomoro • Sartène • Aullène • Zicavo • Santa-Maria-Siché • Ajaccio

This is a long and tiring tour, which is best divided into two days — the western side one day and the scenic D69 another. The country roads and the D69 are very narrow and bumpy. All roads are winding, and driving will be slow. Watch out for foraging animals. Motorcyclists and moped riders should carry extra fuel; some of the rural petrol stations don't have the mixture for mopeds. Reckon on 250km/155mi, 10h driving; take Exit B from Ajaccio (plan page 8).

On route: Walk 3

This drive is brim-full of magnificent country scenery and at its best in spring, when the meadows are saturated with wild flowers and the trees are freshly green. You dip in and out of gentle farmed valleys

Sartène terraces a steep hillside. It is one of Corsica's most 'traditional' towns, where matters of honour and the vendetta were much in evidence for longer then anywhere else on the island. The place is now best known for its Good Friday Procession du Castenacciu, a three hour-long parade of hooded penitents through candle-lit streets, which harks back to medieval times. Climb the steps and wander through the back streets and alleys, sampling the delights of this living history book. The museum of Corsican pre-history houses a wide collection of objects dating back to 6000BC (of particular interest if you visit any sites on this tour). The tree-shaded Place de la Libération is at the heart of the town: here are the town hall (formerly the palace of the Genoese governor) and the 18th-century Eglise Ste-Marie.

interrupted by rocky hills. But as usual, it's the mountain landscape that lures you on: the cosy, welcoming perched villages, the vast cover of trees cloaking the slopes, and the far-reaching views as you climb higher and higher, up to where the shepherds graze their flocks. Also on route lie Filitosa and Sartène, two very different glimpses of Corsica's turbulent history — a prehistoric site and a town that clings to tradition.

Leave Ajaccio by Exit B, the main south route, and follow the N196 towards Propriano. You cross the Prunelli River and climb to the **Col St-Georges** (29km ▲✕🕿). Walk 3 sets off from the inn here. Once over the pass, you look out over an enormous basin of low rolling valleys. Silvery-green olive trees stand out amid evergreen oaks. Cross the Taravo River and soon the woods give way to fields. Pass through **Casalabriva** (57km ▲▲✕), then, 1.8km further on, leave the N196: turn sharp right on a narrow country road to **Sollacaro**, an appealing, rustic village steeped in history. Literature buffs may be interested to know that Dumas' novel, *The Corsican Brothers* (which incidentally has little to do with the island), came out of his short sojourn here in 1841. Boswell also spent some time here in 1765, in the company of Paoli, one of Corsica's great freedom fighters. Just through Sollacaro bear sharp left on the D57, down to an undulating plain spread out along the Taravo delta amidst brightly-coloured spring flowers.

If you're not 'into' history, you won't find the insubstantial **Station Préhistorique de Filitosa★** (68km 🚻▲▲ ✕M) overly exciting. However, compensation enough for nature lovers is the site's picturesque setting and the

Porto-Vecchio: the citadel, seen from the port

profusion of wild flowers in spring, especially the clusters of purple orchids. Filitosa is the island's most important prehistoric settlement and amazingly, this site remained undetected for nearly 5000 years. An avenue of pines leads you to the *menhirs* (stone-carved mega-lithic 'statues' that resemble standing mummies). Cork and olive trees beautify the site, and cows graze nearby. If you can read French, you'll find the small museum here of interest.

Following the Taravo, you head towards a coastline sprinkled with holiday homes and tourist hamlets. Your view extends across the Golfe de Valinco to a long inviting stretch of sand at the foot of the Taravo hills — the Plage de Portigliolo. This will be your 'beach stop' later in the tour. Propriano is just across the bay now. Unfortunately, the terminal disease of tourism is already beginning to eat away at the setting. Some 5km before the town, you rejoin the N196 and circle behind the beach at **Propriano** (86.5km ▲▲▲△✕🖳⊕). You can either visit the town or bypass it by following signs for Porto-Vecchio. Just beyond the Rizzanèse River, leave the N196 and bear right on the D121, towards the coast. Passing Propriano's Tavaria Aerodrome, the road skirts the superb Plage de Portigliolo, the long beach that you could see from across the bay. A low ridge of sand rises off the aquamarine sea and folds over into green fields. You can park at the end of the beach.

Crossing the hills for Campomoro, you get a stunning panorama over this clear sweeping bay and onto the distant encircling hills. Shortly, the tiny village of **Belvé-dère** is reached. Perfectly named, this hillside perch has an enviable view (☎) straight out over the harbour. From here continue to **Campomoro** (102km 🏠▲▲△✕), a seaside village set around a shallow beach. A Genoese tower adorns a nearby promontory. New settlement on the maquis-covered hillsides is slowly eroding Campomoro's 'off-the-beaten-track' appeal.

Return to Belvédère and continue straight ahead, along the D221. You enter an isolated (not to say bleak) countryside drenched in scrub. Bypass Grossa, a handful of stone houses set back off the road. Further on, you circle some farms well ensconced in these wavy hills. The landscape is beautifully untamed, rocky and woven in maquis. Put your head out of the car window and smell the fragrance — a mixture of *Cistus,* lavender and thorny broom. The D21 carries you to a

T-junction with the D48. Tizzano (and two prehistoric sites) are to the right. Personally, I found Tizzano (⌂ ▲▲ ✖) overrated in many guides, and the main tour doesn't visit it. But you may wish to make a detour to the sites.*

Turn left on the D48 and left again on meeting the N196. Mounting a crest, you come to an excellent panorama over the Rizzanèse Valley's basin of trees and fields. The town of **Sartène★** (127km ✝▲▲▲⚠✖ ⊕M; notes and photograph page 23) terraces a steep hillside. Coming into town, you pass the imposing San Damiano Monastery (✝) and look over a hillside fortified with tall stone buildings. Sartène commands a fine view over the Rizzanèse Valley.

If the day hasn't passed you by, from Sartène make for the D69: follow the N196 towards Ajaccio and turn right on the D268 for Ste-Lucie-de-Tallano. But don't forget to look back on Sartène! Just over 4km along, on your left, you'll see the beautifully-arched **Spin'a Cavallu★** (the 'Horse's Back'; ▣), a 13th-century Genoese bridge. Heading inland, you pass pastures knee-high in grass and speckled with red, purple and yellow flowers. On reaching the first junction, bear left onto the D69 for Aullène, crossing the Rizzanèse River.

An intriguing countryside opens up before you. The Rizzanèse twists its way through the central massif. A few lone houses enjoy the solitude of this cut-off valley. Small stone bridges and the ever-present wild flowers add to the countryfied charm. A T-junction suddenly appears, and here you bear left for **Aullène** (162.5km ▲▲✖🍴). Set amidst chestnut groves and silhouetted against a cone-shaped mountain, this village curves around the crest of a ridge.

From Aullène follow signs for Zicavo. Leaving the trees behind, you climb into cowherds' domain, a bleak, rocky landscape with meagre pastureland scattered amongst the heather-clad slopes. Humble farm dwellings have been converted into attractive summer retreats. Crossing a pass, the **Col de la Vaccia** (▣), you

---

*Take the D48 towards Tizzano. Some 8km down turn left (signposted 'Cauria'). After 4.5km bear right (signposted 'Dolmen'). Follow the motorable track for another 0.8km: the dolmen is on your right, beyond a stile. Return to the D48 and bear left. After 2.1km, turn right up a dirt track (*just* past the vineyards; signposted 'Menhirs de Palaggiu'). Leave your car in the parking area and follow the track, soon bearing left. Over 250 of these monoliths are in the area. But the site itself has only a small number of them, standing all in a line ... rather like drunken sailors, each in a different state of collapse.

You don't have to be a mountaineer to enjoy walking on Corsica. Many walks take you into gentle countryside. This golden valley lies below Tralonca (Walk 20) and is visited in one of the Short walk suggestions on page 14.

have a wonderful view back across this elevated valley onto Aullène, comfortably set in the woodlands below. To the west lies the deep Taravo Valley and, all around you, a choppy sea of hills and mountains. Descending, you come into splendid beech woods; under the evening sun the leaves glow and the hills come alight. Around here, be sure to search the roadside for exquisite mountain anemones. Their colour varies from off-white or pale mauve to blue. You may also spot the almost fluorescent *Helleborus*.

Cross over a roaring cascade just before entering **Zicavo** (188.5km 🏔✕). Bear left as you come into the top of the village. A narrow wooded gorge leads you out of this enclosed valley, and you briefly follow the Taravo River once more. At the junction 4km downhill, swing sharp left for Ajaccio. Some 2.4km further on, just as you pass through the pretty tree-lined village of **Bains de Guitera** (🏔✕🏠), fork right onto the D83 (at 195km). Climbing up through forested valleys, you cross yet another pass. Rustic, shuttered villages, all picturesquely located, lie along your homeward route: some cling to ridges, some adorn prominent crags, and some shelter in hollows.

A couple of kilometres before rejoining the N196 come to fields and the farming village of **Sta-Maria-Siché** (216km 🏛🏔✕🏠). Keep an eye out for the 15th-century Château d'Ornano, set in the trees just below the village. Once back on the N196, a straight run of 34km takes you to Ajaccio.

Calvi 1: THE ISOLATED NIOLO BASIN AND THE BREATH-TAKING WESTERN GULFS

Calvi • l'Ile-Rousse • Ponte Leccia • Francardo • Calacuccia • Evisa • Gorges de Spelunca • Ota • Calvi

Driving will be slow: there are stretches of rough, patched roads all the way. The entire route is winding and often narrow. Always be on the alert for foraging animals! The weather can be cold and cloudy, since much of the route is quite high. The Col de Vergio may be closed in bad weather. There are no petrol stations between l'Ile-Rousse and Ponte Leccia (41km) or Calacuccia and Porto (51km). Moped riders must carry extra petrol, since there is no mixture at Calacuccia. Because this is such a long drive, I have not included les Calanche on this tour. Keep aside another full day for exploring the environs of Porto Gulf, and use the notes for 'Ajaccio 1' to tour that area. For this excursion, reckon on 234km/145mi, about 8h30min driving; take exit A from Calvi (plan page 9).

On route: *P* (see pages 11-14): 9, 12, 16; ⌂ at les Cascades d'Aitone; Walks 8, 9, 10, 12, 13, 16, 17, 18

Crossing the island's central spine of mountains, you pass through the isolated Niolo Basin, home of shepherds and herdsmen. On your return to the west coast, you climb to the Col de Vergio, the highest road pass on Corsica. You can cool off in the fresh limpid pools of the Spelunca or Aitone gorges, before descending to the beautiful gulfs of Porto and Girolata.

From Calvi take the N197 (the main north road for l'Ile-Rousse and Bastia; Exit A). Crossing the plain you look up to the pretty hillside village of Lumio★ (9.5km ♨▲▲▲△✕), terracing the hills of the Capu d'Occi and the Capu Bracajo. It commands a fine view over the Calvi Gulf and the citadel. Pass 'Chez Charles' (where Walk 13 begins) and, at the junction, bear left on the N197 to continue along the coast. You look down onto Marine de Sant' Ambrogio (▲▲△✕), a classy resort. Pass above Algajola (16km ◻♨▲▲▲△✕🍴), another burgeoning resort, at the end of a curving bay. Its Genoese fort is in ruins, except for the citadel. Inland Monte Grosso dominates the great wall of mountains.

You pass several roads leading inland to the Balagne (Car tour 'Calvi 3'). Then, just outside l'Ile-Rousse, you see the striking (and least spoilt) beach along this stretch of coast, the Plage de Botre, sitting off the turquoise-blue Baie de Guinchetu. All you see of **l'Ile-Rousse** (23km ♨▲▲▲△✕🍴⊕🛒WC) is a street lined with plane trees. Save your visit to this very pleasant town for a cloudy or wet afternoon. Better still, save it for the day you do Walk 13, which ends here.

Further along the coast your views extend to the

28

more rugged shore line of the Désert des Agriates and, in the distance, Cap Corse. Turning inland, you circle an extensive sandy beach at **Lozari** (30km 🏨🏠⛺🍴). Keep right at the St-Florent/Bastia intersection, continuing on the N197. The road winds above the wide-slung Regino Valley and then the Prato Valley. Hayfields square off the plains. Circling the imposing church of St-Thomas, you swing in and out of **Belgodère** (38km ⛪🏨🏠🍴WC). Almost nothing remains of the fortress that once crowned the rocky outcrop here. However, it's a fine viewing point for the Prato Valley (📷).

You leave behind the dishevelled, scrubby countryside and climb into large round hills. The Barrage de Codole, a wide expanse of water set back in the Regino Valley, catches your eye, just before you disappear into a desolate landscape. Palasca is the severe-looking village below the road, huddled round its church. Over these hills, you drop down into a narrow valley and wind alongside a small stream lined with poplars and plane trees. Soon the mountains enshrouding the Asco Valley (see tour 'Calvi 2') burst up on your right.

Come to **Ponte Leccia** (64km 🏨🏠⛺🍴🚉), an important junction for the north, and join the N193. Carry on to **Francardo** (73km 🏨🍴). Just outside this village, turn off right on the D84 for Calacuccia, following the Golo, Corsica's most important river. Recrossing the river,

Car tour Calvi 3: Climbing towards the Bocca di a Battaglia, en route for Olmi-Cappela, a magnificent panorama unravels. You look down over Speloncato to the wide open Regino Valley and Lozari's luminous green bay.

bear left. You enter a magnificent gorge, the **Scala di Sta Regina★**, a winding passageway that links the Niolo with the east. Rocky hillsides tumble off the towering mountain chain that rises some 1000m/3300ft on either side. Approaching the **Niolo★**, the gorge opens out, and rough pastures appear. Remains of stone walls, footbridges, and solitary huts speak of grazing land.

Just before you enter Calacuccia, fork left on the D218, signposted for Casamaccioli, and circle the picturesque Barrage de Calacuccia. You cross the dam wall and look over the reservoir to the amphitheatre of rocky mountains that encloses this high basin. Sloping pastures lie between the scattering of sheltered hamlets and the crags. Monte Cinto (Corsica's highest peak at 2706m/8875ft) stands out with its ramp-shaped summit. **Casamaccioli** (97km 🛉🏠) is a pretty village set back off the wooded banks of the lake. Each year on the 8th of September, the most important festival on the island is held here (the Nativity of the Virgin). All the shepherds return from the mountains with their flocks for this three-day fête; if you are in the area, don't miss it!

The pool at the Refuge de Sega (Walk 21) is a favourite swimming spot for those really fit hikers who can make the most of Corsica's mountain walks.

At the T-junction just inside Casamaccioli, bear right and continue around the lake, a lovely place to picnic. Returning to **Calacuccia** (102km ♦♠♣✕🍽), bear left and pass through it. The village is quite ordinary, but is superbly sited overlooking the lake. In the church there is an interesting 17th-century wooden statue of Christ; the carving is particularly expressive. Continuing on the D84, you pass below a 17th-century Franciscan monastery (♦) set back in the trees. Beyond **Albertacce** (104km ♠♠ and M of archaeology) you cross the Golo for the last time. Note the small footbridge below left and the pretty gorge cutting back up to the right.

As you head across the plateau, the landscape becomes noticeably rocky and is clad in trees and bushes. Soon pines take over, and you're in the **Forêt de Valdu Niellu★**, Corsica's largest forest. Some of these pencil-straight trees reach a height of 50m/165ft. Pull over at a roadside viewpoint (📷), to look back down the bowl-shaped Golo Valley to the dam. Still climbing, come to the ski station and the highest hotel on the island (♠♠✕). Approaching the **Col de Vergio★** (📷; 1404m/4605ft), you catch a glimpse of the Punta Licciola and, behind it, the 'pierced' summit of Capu Tafunatu. From the pass there are more splendid views towards the Licciola peak and other bare summits, all lightly flecked with a luminous green lichen, and down over the Golo.

Over the pass, the Aitone Valley winds its way seaward. The **Cascades d'Aitone★** (🏕), 7.5km down from the pass, make a good cooling-off, stretch-your-legs stop. The turn-off, to the right, is not far beyond the forestry house you see below the road (a small sign, 'Piscine/les Cascades', stands at the entrance to this track). Bump your way along to the tired picnic tables and parking area of sorts; then explore. The river drops down over shelves of rock just before the valley closes up into a sheer-sided ravine. There is an excellent viewpoint over this gorge some 100m further along the D84. Go there on foot, following the orange-paint dashes along the road (leave your car where it is, in the 'Cascades' car park). At the first bend in the road (where there is a pole with paint on its tip), turn off through a fenced-off area. A five-minute walk leads to a rocky spur that hangs out over the gorge (📷).

Out of the forest, you enter chestnut groves. Bear right at the junction and head for **Evisa** (130km ♠♠♣ △✕), a charming mountain village. An agreeable retreat in the hot summer months, Evisa is also well placed for exploring the interior and the Porto Gulf area. Walk 9 sets out from here. Just beyond the cemetery, a roadside balcony (📷) affords a splendid view of Ota, perched high in the walls of the deep Porto Valley. The rocky hillsides here blush pink, and pinnacles of rock burst up out of the surrounding walls. The road curls down into a side valley thick with chestnut trees. Keep right past two turn-offs left for Marignana (where Walk 8 begins); then, 14km from Evisa, turn back sharp right onto the D124 for Ota. You soon cross the Porto River, at the mouth of the **Gorges de Spelunca★**. A path on your right, just before you cross the first bridge, follows the Aitone River up into a spectacular wooded gorge (**P**9 at the Pont de Zaglia; photograph page 82). This area is the setting for Walk 9. A few hundred metres beyond 'les Deux Ponts d'Ota' ('Ota's Two Bridges'), you look down onto a lovely, high-arched Genoese foot-bridge, the **Ponte Vecchiu★** (📷). The river here is ideal for swimming; it's another lovely picnic setting (**P**9).

This rough road has carried us to **Ota** (148km 🏨 🏠 ✕ 📷), the colourful village with bright orange-tiled rooftops shown on page 84. A lofty ridge capped in rose-coloured rock looms above it. Walk 9 ends here, and Walk 10 begins here. Leaving the valley, you come down to the tourist village of Porto (Tour 'Ajaccio 1'). This tour doesn't enter Porto; instead, bear right at the junction, onto the D81. From here you have a superb **view of Porto★** and its spectacular setting. The rock dome of the Capu d'Ortu, behind you, stands guard over the bay. Superb seascapes open up over the head-

Les Calanche, a wonderland of rock pinnacles (Walk 11, Picnic 11)

lands. The twin-headed Monte Seninu rises straight up out of the sea, dramatically punctuating the end of the gulf. A vast beach, the Plage de Bussaglia (🏔🏠△✕), appears below.

Continue along the corniche to the **Bocca a Croce★**. This pass is not signposted, so watch for a cross on your left, 1.3km beyond the Osani turn-off. Pull over to the parking area *carefully* (dangerous corner) and continue on foot to the viewpoint (📷). The pretty cove of Girolata sits tucked back in a striking stretch of coast. Short walk 18 (highly recommended) leads from this pass to Girolata via the Anse de Tuara, an exquisite cove (notes page 106; photograph page 108).

Walk 18 ends here on the D81, not far south of the Col de Palmarella. Over the pass, you descend into the flat-bottomed Fango Valley (🚌). The Fango is the setting for Walks 16 and 17 so, when you tire of beaches, drive up into this peaceful valley one day, find yourself your own rock pool, and enjoy a lazy day of swimming, sunning and picnicking (*P*16). This unbelievably lovely setting, with a riverbed ranging in colour from pink to purple, and blue and green river pools, is a particular favourite of mine (see photograph page 103).

Galéria (4km from the Calvi junction; 🏨🏔🏠△✕) is another village being nibbled away by tourism. If you have time, head along the D351 (🚌) as far as the parking area (3km, on the right, just below the tower). Then walk down to the enticing beach at the mouth of the Fango, with its pretty lagoon and enchanting coppice.

The main tour continues on the D81 by crossing the Fango; you reach a junction and bear left along the longer, but more lovely coastal route (D81b), with fine views back over the Golfe de Galéria. Coming into **l'Argentella** (211km 🏔△✕), you look out over the Baie de Crovani. L'Argentella sits on the edge of an open valley, sheltered by a sweeping curve of rocky hills. Back along the coast, your views reach to la Revellata, the arm of land with the lighthouse (Alternative walk 12). Having rounded the turquoise-green Baie de Nichiareto, you enjoy an amazing vista of fat rocky mountains in shades of pink, orange and grey.

Looking out over the jagged sea cliffs serrating the southern coastline, you enter the outskirts of Calvi under the setting sun. Along the way, pass the turn-off to the church of **Notre Dame de la Serra★** (⛪📷*P*12; photograph page 91), one of the settings for Walk 12.

Calvi 2: THE ASCO VALLEY

Calvi • l'Ile-Rousse • Belgodère • Haut Asco • Asco • Calvi

The road is good as far as the Asco turn-off, but winding beyond l'Ile-Rousse. The D147 to Asco is rough, patched, and narrows to only one lane in places. You may not be able to get as far as Haut Asco in early spring or late autumn. It can also be very cold and misty on this high road. Watch for foraging animals. Ponte Leccia, 2km beyond the Asco turn-off, is your last chance for petrol for 62km. Reckon on 188km/117mi, 7h driving; take exit A from Calvi (plan page 9).

On route: Walk 13

The Asco Valley is one of those gorges that disappears into the interior mountains and then stops dead in its tracks at the foot of towering crags. Paths to attract the curious and energetic abound here, so take a picnic lunch and spend an hour or two somewhere on the edge of the beautiful river that keeps you company all the way up. Then, before the sun has lost its warmth, head back to the Genoese bridge below Asco and revive yourself in the blue-green pool that it spans. Shake the ice off and make for Calvi under a dying sun.

Follow the notes for Tour 'Calvi 1' all the way to the turn-off for the **Gorges de l'Asco★** (62km; 2km north of Ponte Leccia). Bear right (D47) and, 5km further on, left onto the D147. Soon great salients of rock loom above. Further along, the abruptness subsides, and the walls lean back to reveal side valleys. Asco (79km) soon comes into sight, built on terraces in the steep valley wall. Without entering the village, swing up right to the ski station. You come into a magnificent pine forest, the Forêt de Carozzica, as you skirt the gushing Stranciacone River (many good picnic spots and room to park).

Haut Asco (93km ▲▲▲✕), the ski station, is a bit of an eyesore, but the surrounding alpine scenery is enchanting. The best thing to do is scramble up the slopes until the hotel is out of sight! A breathtaking 30-minute climb takes you past grand Corsican pines and up onto a plateau strewn with pink- and mauve-coloured rock, amongst the foothills of **Monte Cinto★**.

If you fancy a dip in the pool below Asco, on your return bear right for the village (first right over the bridge) and, almost immediately, go right again to zigzag down a tarred lane to the pool and bridge. Return via **Asco**, a village dating from the 11th century. Make for home the same way, or try the 'roller coaster' D47 via **Multifao**: at the T-junction with the D547, bear left and cross the Capanna Pass to descend to the N197.

Calvi 3: VILLAGES OF THE BALAGNE, AND THE TARTAGINE VALLEY

Calvi • **Calenzana** • **Muro** • **Speloncato** • **Bocca di a Battaglia** • **Tartagine Valley** • **Belgodère** • **l'Ile-Rousse** • **Corbara** • **Sant' Antonino** • **Lumio** • Calvi

The whole tour follows narrow, winding and bumpy roads. Watch out for foraging animals, especially between Speloncato and Belgodère. There are no petrol stations between Cateri and l'Ile-Rousse (98km). The Bocca di a Battaglia might be closed in early spring or late autumn in bad weather. Reckon on 161km/100mi; 6h driving; take exit A from Calvi (plan page 9).

On route: **P** (see pages 11-14): 13; Walks 13, 14. Walk 15 and Picnic 15 are accessible from Calenzana via the D51, but are best reached via the airport road (D81) and then the D251 direct to Bonifatu.

The Balagne is a region full of charming villages, each with a different personality. Every one seems to have its own baroque church, and all have a balcony view over the plains and hills that characterise the area. Stopping at all of them is impossible, and choosing between them a difficult task. I'll leave that to you. Over the hills, behind this salubrious countryside, lies a quiet, cut-off valley that few people visit, the Tartagine. Its beautiful pine and evergreen oak forests, and the finely-etched Monte Padro, make another lovely circuit, before you return through the Balagne to Calvi.

Follow the N197 (Exit A) as far as the Calenzana turn-off, 4.5km out of town. Turn right on the D151 for **Calenzana** (12.5km ✝🏔🏔▲△✕🏠); it sits out of sight in a flat valley amidst olive and almond trees, with its back to the prominent Monte Grosso (1938m/6355ft). Calenzana verges on being a town, with its maze of alleys, gardens and shops. It's an important agricultural centre, noted for ewes-milk cheese (*brocciu*), wine, and *charcutérie*. The 17th/18th-century baroque church of St-Blaise dwarfs the village centre, and its elegant campanile enhances the square. Walk 14 begins here.

Just 1km outside the village, still on the D151, you pass the tiny church dedicated to Ste-Restitute (✝), a Corsican martyr beheaded by the Romans in 303. The road winds deeper into the Fiume Seccu Valley, through untidy countryside crammed with olive, oak, cherry and chestnut trees. Barely 7km from Calenzana, you cross a bridge (🚱 by a stream to the right).

An enchanting old stone church stands above the road in **Lunghignano** (22km ✝✕). **Montemaggiore** (23.5km ✝🍷) adorns a prominent rocky ridge jutting out into the Fiume Seccu. It commands a fine view over

35

Calvi's gulf. A kilometre out of the village, just where the D151 swings up left, take the dirt track branching off right, to the simple Romanesque Church of St-Rainer (✝, 12th century), resting in fields. Back on the main road and climbing into *Cistus*-covered hills, you have expansive views over the settings for Walk 12: the plains below, the Calvi Gulf, la Revellata, and the hills of rock that enclose the Figarella Valley. Then, crossing the **Bocca di Salvi★** (🚐), you look down into the Algajola Basin, chequered with fields. Sant' Antonino is perched high on the crest of a ridge ahead.

On meeting an intersection (🚐), bear right on the D71 for Muro. The sickle-shaped Codole Reservoir stretches out in the floor of the Regino Valley. After 4km, turn right into **Muro** (33km ✝✕🚐); you arrive at the door of the imposing church, the Eglise de l'Annonciation, one of the finest examples of the baroque style on Corsica. Continue past the church to leave Muro and bear right again on the D71. **Feliceto** (39km 🏔✕) is surrounded by orchards. Leave the D71 when the way forks and turn right (D663) for **Speloncato** (45km ✝🏔▲✕🚐). This strategically-sited village is built on a high outcrop of rock, overlooking the Regino Basin.

From here you ascend for some fine views over **the Balagne★**. Squeezing through the narrow streets, take the narrow Olmi-Cappela road (D63) out of Speloncato. Climb past a derelict monastery and the view shown on page 29 to the **Bocca di a Battaglia★** (🚐🅿). Here an even more stupendous panorama unfolds — over the reservoir, Speloncato, the embroidery of fields in the Regino Valley, the luminous green Lozari Bay, the arid Désert des Agriates, Cap Corse, and the red Ile-Rousse.

You drop down into a tree-flooded valley. On reaching the D963 turn sharp right, then keep right for the rest of the way. A bumpy road winds its way high above isolated Melaja and **Tartagine★** valleys. Monte Padro (2390m/7840ft) dominates the landscape on your left. Beyond the shuttered forestry house, cross the Tartagine, a healthy stream with knee-deep pools. The road ends at private property (parking area in shade at the left), but enticing paths lead into the forest.

Turn back along the D963 and continue straight through Olmi-Cappela, to join the N197. Turn left for l'Ile-Rousse and pass above Palasca, a lonely village nestled round its church. You might like to visit the imposing 13th-century Church of St-Thomas at **Belgodère**

(112km ⬚♦✕◐WC), another strategically-sited village. From the scant remains of the fortress that once dominated the settlement, you look down over the Regino and Prato valleys. Circling down above the fertile plains, you pass the turn-off to Regino and Lozari's tempting beach. Head straight through **l'Ile-Rousse** (128km ♦⛰ ⛰△✕⚑◐WC); it deserves a visit, but is easily accessible by train from Calvi. Walk 13 ends here. Some 1.5km out of town, bear right (signposted 'Calvi') and then go left immediately on the D151 for Corbara. From the hillside, the Baie de Guinchetu and the Plage de Botre look enticing. Bear left again, at the next fork.

From the instant you see **Corbara** (132km ♦✕ ◐WC), you know it's going to be different. Palm trees in a garden above the road set the scene. There's a distinct Moorish flavour about the place. From the chapel of Notre Dame (built into the rocky vertex above the village and once the site of the Castel de Corbara), you have fine views over the Algajola Bay to la Revellata. The 18th-century Church of the Annunciation stands guard over the village.

Continuing round the Algajola basin, with good views of Corbara's setting, you soon spot the imposing 15th-century Monastery of Corbara★ (♦) below Monte Sant' Angelo. **Pigna** (134km) crowns a hillock growing out of the valley wall. The village, shown on page 17, is a handicraft centre★, where traditional arts such as weaving, pottery, and woodworking are practised.

A profusion of olive and citrus trees welcomes you to **Aregno** (137km ♦). Visit the little Church of the Trinity (on the D151), to see the humorous figurines decorating the façade and two exquisite 15th-century frescoes. Just 1km beyond Aregno, turn off sharp left (D413) for the 'pièce de résistance' of the Balagne, **Sant' Antonino★** (141km ✕◐*P*13; Walk 13; photograph page 95). Do stop to explore this 9th-century settlement and its treasure-trove of old and restored buildings.

Returning to the D151, head left and, at the junction 500m along, turn right towards Lumio. **Cateri** (144km ♦✕⚑) is one of my favourite villages; the very popular inn here might be the reason (turn off right to reach it). Pass above a monastery on your right and, on meeting the N197, turn left. Beyond **Lumio** (151km ⛰⛰△✕), the second left-hand turn leads to the 11th-century Romanesque San Pietro Church (♦), with its curious lion-headed portal. Calvi is straight on.

Bastia • Rogliano • Centuri-Port • Nonza • St-Florent • Bastia

Roads on the east coast are good; those on the west are narrow and often bumpy. All are winding. Be on the alert for livestock on the roadside along the west coast. Reckon on 137km/85mi, 5h driving, take exit A from Bastia (plan page 10).

On route: 🍴 at Nonza; Walk 19

C ap Corse stands apart from the rest of Corsica, both geographically and scenically. Contrasting coastal landscapes accompany you all the way on this tour: the east is gentle and subdued; the west sharp and dramatic. Watchtowers litter the countryside, and monasteries are as common as churches. Vestiges of the past lie around every corner. Small coves, some sandy, some pebbly, will draw you down to the magnetic turquoise sea. This excursion can be split into a leisurely two-day outing, the east coast one day, the west another.

Heading north on the D80 (Exit A) past **Pietranera** (3km 🏨🍴🏪) and **Miomo** (5.5km 🅿🏨⛺🍴), you're still in residential confines. Posh villas in choice locations overlook the sea. Pass the turn-off left for Pozzo, starting point for the ascent of **Monte Stello★**. At 1307m/4285ft, this is the highest summit on the cape (Walk 19). **Lavasina** (⛪🏨🍴) is the site of one of the island's most important festivals (the Nativity of the Virgin, celebrated on the 8th September). The 17th-century church, Notre Dame des Graces (with an unsightly campanile) houses a painting of the Virgin and Child which is revered by fishermen and attributed with miraculous powers. The short (but still pretty stiff!) version of Walk 19 begins just by this church and takes you to the church at Pozzo, shown on page 110.

Before coming into **Erbalunga★** (10km 🅿🏨⛪🍴), a favourite haunt of artists, you will spot it — a group of houses crammed onto a low spit of rock, sitting out in the water. The houses appear to 'grow' out of the sea. You can wander through the alleys of this curious old fishing village in five minutes. Four kilometres beyond Erbulunga, a balcony (📷) juts out of the hillside below the road. A tiny, rather special rocky cove sits out of sight to the right of it. It's an ideal swimming spot.

If you can chase up the key for the parish Church of St Martin up in the Commune de Sisco (enquire in advance at the Syndicat d'Initiative in Bastia), you may like to look over its hoard of treasures: the bit of soil from which God made Adam, hairs from the cloak of St John the Baptist, and a fragment of a coat worn by the Virgin Mary ... to mention but a few. The turn-off for Sisco (D32) is at **Marine de Sisco** (15.5km ▲▲△✕). Once in **Sisco** (7km uphill), you'll have another search for the key to the simple, ideally-sited Romanesque San Michele Chapel (♣), not far above St-Martin (♣). To get there, bear right past St-Martin and take the first left, up a rough track. Come to another fork: park, and walk up to the right. Continue along an overgrown path when the track swings left. By the remains of a stone building, bear right along a hillside shelf and, fifteen minutes from the car you're there. Don't worry if you forgot the key; you have really climbed here for the views over the valley and across the sea to the islands off Tuscany.

Return to the coastal road through this lush tree-rich landscape, where hamlets of stone-built houses huddle in the shade. Turn left and continue for another 2km, as far as the turn-off for the Convent of Santa Catalina (signposted 'Manoir Santa Catalina'). This monastery (♣) is now an old people's home and occupies a fine perch overlooking the sea. Beautifully restored, it has an imposing fortified tower. Only the dilapidated church is open to the public (key obtained in the home).

The countryside loses its trees; the turquoise-blue of the sea deepens. **Marine de Pietracorbara** (20km ▲▲ ✕⌂), a pleasant resort of white sand set back in a U in the coast, boasts the first substantial beach you reach. The well-preserved Tour de l'Osse (⌂) serves as a particularly striking landmark, further along the coast. A pretty pebbly cove lies just below it. **Porticciolo** (26km ▲▲✕) is a small village overlooking the sea. A tiny marina and narrow beach shelter in its shallow bay.

Come to **Santa Severa** (28km ▲△✕🚾). From here you can take a detour (not on the main tour) to explore the lovely Luri Valley, fresh with greenery.* The main tour continues straight along the D80, past an unspoilt shingle beach, before reaching the spread-out seaside village of **Marine de Meria** (34km ⌂▲▲). Some four

*Turn left inland on the D180. The first village en route is Piazza (♣), where the church holds a 15th-century painting on its altar screen depicting the life of St Peter. Beyond Luri (▲▲), at the Col de Ste-Lucie (🚌), a side road leads off left to an orphanage (the Maison d'Enfants de Luri), 1km uphill. The children here run a small museum (M) which they have stocked from their own archeological finds in the area, especially around the Tour de Sénèque★, the remains of the Genoese tower crowning the nearby crag (⌂).

kilometres further on lies the small fishing port of **Macinaggio** (38.5km ⛺△✕🏠). It sits at the end of a long sandy beach, which is excellent for the children.

Continuing west, leave the D80 some 4km beyond Macinaggio: turn left (D53) for the historic **Commune de Rogliano★** (⛺). This settlement of eight hamlets dominates the surrounding hills with its large number of prominent buildings, arousing your curiosity long before you reach it. In **Bettolacce** (44.5km 🛈✝⛺✕🍴), you come face to face with the Eglise St-Agnel, set high on the hillside, from where there is a superb view down over Macinaggio. Below the church sits the Chapel of the Confrèrie de Ste-Croix and below that, the impressive Tour Franceschi, standing guard over the hamlet. Passing through Bettolacce, return to the D80, remembering to look back at the scattering of mottled-grey houses ensconced amongst the trees. The ruins of the Convent of St Francis (✝) are glimpsed on a hilltop above, and the view over Macinaggio's bay is superb.

Bear left on the D80, to look straight off the end of the cape to the sharp islet of la Giraglia. Winding around quiet scrub-covered hills, you pass the Tollare/Barcaggio junction (from where you can take a detour of 15.5km on a very bumpy road to the curving sandy beach of Barcaggio (⛺✕). The main tour continues on the D80, passing the intersection and climbing to the **Col de la Serra** (📷). From here you can also walk (30min return) to the Moulin Mattei★, an excellent viewpoint over the cape (take the first track off right).

Once over the pass, the more dramatic western coast unfolds before you (📷). Sheer hills rise straight up out of the sea. Villages nestle on protruding ridges. Turn off sharp right onto the D35 at **Camera** (50km), squeezing through the hamlet. Soon a medieval-style château is passed (🏛), set amidst trees in a garden below the road. This building belonged to General Cipriani (19thC). Head left at the fork beyond the château and wind down through olive trees and evergreen oaks. Come to a junction overlooking the scrub-covered Ilôt de Centuri, and turn right for **Centuri-Port★** (54.5km 🛈⛺△✕). Parking in the village is sheer hell, since a one-way system operates, but this port is definitely worth a stop. Lobsters are the speciality of the local fishermen, so if you feel like splurging, now is the time.

From Centuri-Port, remain on the D35, keeping straight ahead for **Morsiglia** (59km). Some large rotund

watch-towers dot the hills. Rejoining the D80, you head
south around the seaside slopes. Shortly, a stunning
bay, the Aliso Gulf, shines up at you. The grey collar of
rock intensifies the contrast of forest-green vegetation
and a crystalline blue sea. A steep rough track goes
down to the beach, but it's best reached on foot.

Should you wish to make a detour to the orphanage
mentioned in the footnote on page 39 (**M**), take the
turn-off left (D180) signposted for Luri/Santa Severa, just
outside **Pino** (69km ⛪🏔✕🍴📷). Pino is a gracious
hillside village, its houses scattered amidst a profusion
of trees: cypress, palms, planes, oaks and olives. Look
back to see sheer coastal ridges toppling off into the
sea. The Convent of St Francis (⛪🏠), more impressive
when seen from above, perches on a rocky shore down
to the right. (The road to it forks off just a kilometre
beyond Pino.) While the old convent now houses a
private school, there is an interesting fresco in the
chapel and a Genoese tower in the grounds.

The coastline becomes more exciting as you continue on towards St-Florent. The D80 hangs out over
sea cliffs that drop away into the indigo depths. Strips of
overgrown terracing step stretches of near-vertical
slopes; prickly-pear cactus is in its element. You pass
through an outburst of jagged ridges and then curve
inland up the Furcone Valley. Below is the Marine de
Giottani, another pretty cove set in white rock. It
quickly opens up into an irresistibly dazzling little
beach. Most people drive past it slowly and, a minute
later, stop the car, turn round and go back to it. High
above the sea again, an enormous building (which at
first glance you might mistake for an hotel) disrupts the
seascape. It's an abandoned asbestos mine. If you can
ignore this awesome sight, you will enjoy the tremendous view across the hilly coastline towards the central
massif and the bumpy Désert des Agriates. Black sand
beaches lie below you here, further intensifying another
colour contrast: white rock and royal-blue sea.

Your approach to **Nonza★** (94.5km 📷⛪🏔✕📷) is
spectacular. Its captivating beach, a long wide band of
pebbles made almost inaccessible by the sheer-sided
hills that rise up out of it, spans out directly below you.
The village is superbly sited, built into a rocky spur that
leans out over the tail of the beach some 150m/500ft
below. A tower, marking the site of a medieval fort,
crowns the spur: this is an awe-inspiring perch and a

delightful place to unpack the picnic basket. You have stupendous views down onto the beach and over the orange, lichen-covered slate roof-tops of the village, splashed with purple bougainvillaea. Nonza was the birthplace of Saint Julie, a martyr crucified by the Romans for her Christian beliefs. A pilgrimage to the Fountain of St Julie and its altar is held each year on the 22nd of May. If you find the tower perch a little too precarious for your picnic lunch, this altar and the two gushing fountains make another lovely picnic spot: they are below the road, on the pathway to the beach (keep right at the fork). Nonza's 16th-century church, with a tableau depicting St Julie, is above the road.

Closer to St-Florent, you begin descending. The coastline eases out and is less exciting visually. Some vineyards and orchards soothe your approach. Five kilometres before the town, meet the Bastia junction; keep right on the D81. **St-Florent★** (114km ▮▮♦▲▲▲▲ ✕♥⊕wc) is a very pleasant resort and a favourite with French tourists. Set deep in the gulf, on the banks of the Alisio River, it clusters round a huge citadel that dominates the port. The Genoese part of the town (**Nebbio★**), however, sits 1km further inland. All that remains of it is the 12th-century cathedral church of Santa Maria Assunta, one of the island's masterpieces. (A sister edifice, La Canonica, may be visited during Tour 'Bastia 3'.) The key to this extremely lovely and interesting church is obtainable at the Auberge de l'Europe at the port.

On your return to Bastia, you pass through **Patrimonio** (121km ♦▲▲✕). Just inside the village, turn off left for the 16th-century Eglise St-Martin (♦). While the interior holds nothing of great interest, this elegantly proportioned church, with its graceful steeple, is very photogenic. Before you reach the church, notice the menhir (▮▮) in a garden on your left. Patrimonio is known for its private (as opposed to co-operative) vineyards, where quality, not quantity, is the vintners' aim. You can sample reds, whites, rosés and muscatels.

The **Col de Teghime★** (▨) is the pass that breaches the high hills separating St-Florent from your base. From here there is a grand panorama over the eastern and western side of the cape and, on hazeless days, towards Elba. Finer still are the views from the **Serra di Pigno★** (▨): the signposted turn-off (D338) is on the left, just over the pass; the viewpoint is 4km uphill.

Return to the D81 and descend to Bastia.

Bastia • Ponte Leccia • Corte • Gorges de la Restonica
Corte • Ponte Leccia • Ponte Nuvo • (Murato •
Défilé de Lancone) • Bastia

The road to Corte is good, but the road by the Restonica is very narrow, winding and bumpy — a steep ascent that not all mopeds can handle! Note: there is a restriction on the size of vehicle that can use this road (some camper-vans are considered too wide). There is no barrier railing on this road, which some people will find vertiginous. The detour from Ponte Leccia to Murato and the Défilé de Lancone is equally vertiginous. These narrow roads may be closed in early spring and late autumn. Even if they are open, they are not recommended in bad weather: rock fall is common, and it can be very cold. Watch out for foraging animals. Reckon on 169km/105mi, 6h driving if you return via your outgoing route; add 34km/1h30min if you return by the 'detour route' described. Take exit B from Bastia (plan page 10).

On route: P (see pages 11-14): 22; Walks 20, 21, 22. Walks 5, 6, 7 and Picnics 5, 7 are easily reached from Corte; see footnote page 44.

Who needs beaches when there are rivers as beautiful as the Restonica? This breath-taking gorge merits a day out in everyone's holiday and, whatever you do, don't miss the lakes visited on Walk 22. Young belles struggle up to them in high heels, and babies go up on dad's back; everyone climbs to see the magnetic beauty of these mirror-like lakes. And when the day is ending, you can throw yourselves into one of the many delicious pools that fill the floor of the Restonica.

Follow the N193 (Exit B) all the way to Corte. At **Casamozza** (20km ▲▲▲✕🅿) you leave the coastal plains behind and come into the Golo Valley, a hilly unkempt area with small farm plots stretching across the narrow river flats. Danger signs warn against swimming in the river; they are there for a good reason! At **Ponte Nuvo** (38km 🅿) you pass the D5 to Murato, an optional detour which you may like to take on the homeward leg. The valley opens up: orchards, vineyards and hayfields cover the floor. Pass through **Ponte Leccia** (46km ▲▲▲△✕🅿), the crossroads of the north, and follow the Golo River.

Crossing the San Quilico Pass, you leave the Golo Valley and descend to **Corte★** (70km ■♦▲▲△✕🅿⊕ ▣Mwc), Corsica's university town, set at the confluence of the Tavignano and Restonica, in the shadow of the central massif. The surrounding countryside is pastoral and cleaner of scrub, with straw-coloured hills (see photograph page 27). Corte remains unaffected by tourism; plain, but pleasant tall buildings line the main street. The old quarter terraces a steep hillface, and a

15th-century fortress crowns the summit. Corte is a fine base for walks and drives into the central mountains.*

Your turn-off for **La Restonica**★ is on the south side of Corte, just beyond the Tavignano. Turn right on the D623 and head up alongside the bounding crystal-clear river. Watch out for cows in the middle of the road. Climbing rapidly, you enter pines. Below the road, small inviting river flats, cushioned in grass and ferns and shaded by pines, make splendid picnic spots. Coming into alpine pastures, the pines subside and only a few grand species remain. The road ends at the enchanting **Bergerie de Grottelle** (84.5km ✗P22), a settlement of low stone houses and animal pens. If you're walking up to the lakes (*highly recommended;* see photograph page 121), leave your transport in the parking area.

In hot weather you may want to end the excursion with a dip in one of those inviting pools further down stream, but if it's too cold or you would rather be driving, then take this long 'detour route' back to Bastia (add 34km/1h30min). Turn off the N193 at **Ponte Nuvo** onto the D5 (immediately over the bridge, on the left and signposted for Lento/Bigorno). This ascent, along a very narrow road, affords views back down the Golo. Pass through Lento, a village set back on tree-patched slopes. As you enter Bigorno, the D5 swings left up to a pass, the Bocca di Bigorno★ (🎦), from where there are fine views over the Golo to table-topped Monte San Petrone above the hills of la Castagniccia and Monte Sant' Angelu above Casinca. Over the pass a rolling plateau devoid of life stretches before you; then you descend through hills laced with chestnut groves. Go straight through Murato (✗🍴). You soon spot the 12th-century San Michele Chapel (♦; photograph page 18) on a flat crest. From here you look down onto the Aliso basin, and the Golfe de St-Florent fills in the backdrop. Descending, you come to a roundabout: take the second fork to the right (D62), into the Défilé (Gorge) de Lancone★. You'll get only a glimpse of the gorge on this hair-raising road where everyone toots with anxiety as they round each bend. But a superb view over the green-embroidered plains of Bastia and the Biguglia Lagoon greets you just before you leave the gorge. Turn left on the N193 to Bastia (photograph page 112).

*Walks 20 and 21 are based on Corte, but the marvellous excursions around Venaco and Vizzavona are also easily accessible (Walks 5, 6, 7; P5, 7). See large-scale map on the reverse of the touring map.

Bastia • Ponte Leccia • Morosaglia • la Porta • Piedicroce • Cervione • San Nicolao • Bastia

Narrow, winding, and sometimes bumpy country roads are followed between Ponte Leccia and Moriani. Watch out for foraging livestock. There are no petrol stations between Ponte Leccia and Cervione (85km). Reckon on 172km/107mi, 5h30min driving. Exit B from Bastia (plan page 10).

On route: ⌂ between Cervione and San Nicolao

There are no real 'sights' on this tour; it is simply a most enjoyable day's outing in a landscape bumpy with hills and thick with the chestnut groves that give their name to the region, the Castagniccia. Small rustic villages echo the silence, with their shuttered houses and boarded-up churches. A pleasant surprise along the way: the old roadside fountains have been restored, given names, and gush forth water once again.

Follow Tour 'Bastia 2' to **Ponte Leccia** (46km). Just before crossing the Golo, bear left on the D71 for Morosaglia. Climbing amidst low abrupt hills, you overlook the Golo Valley. The Aig de Popolasca, a high craggy mass, rears up above the far valley wall. Further along to the left the great Rotondo massif is seen. Junipers and pines share the lower slopes; higher up, cork trees stand out with their crusty bark. (You'll often see a large square piece neatly cut out of the trunk. These trees can only be stripped once every seven years.)

Travelling east, you skirt the upper Golo Valley and look out over the hills above Ponte Nuvo (the 'detour route' in Tour 'Bastia 2'). **Morosaglia** (60.5km ✚M) has a claim to fame: Pascal Paoli, one of Corsica's most noted political figures (after Napoleon of course) was born here. His birthplace is a museum (open daily 09.00-12.00; 15.00-18.00). The Romanesque church of Santa Reparata, where he was baptised, sits above the village; his school (the present village school and named for him) is the grand building on the right as you enter the village. It was formerly the Rostino Monastery and a meeting place for members of the Corsican Liberation Movement in the early 18th century. This pretty village lies scattered deep in the hills amongst chestnut groves. The name of the region, **la Castagniccia★**, derives from the Latin word for sweet chestnut. In the past these trees were the mainstay of the local people. Not only was the flour an important part of their diet and the wood used for furniture, farm tools and firewood, but both were bartered for products from other regions.

Beyond Morosaglia, you come to the Col de Prato (☎), and the sea reappears in the distance over the hills. The rugged inland Fium' Altu, a valley of ridges and hills saturated in trees, stretches out before you. Hamlets lie sporadically dispersed across the inclines. Not far below the pass (some 5km from Morosaglia), turn sharp left on a narrow road that swings downhill towards la Porta (signposted). This lovely road (D205) twirls its way round the hillsides under an arcade of trees. The countryside is crisp with arboreal greenery. You squeeze through and then past a couple of old grey hamlets. Faded white arrows and signs painted on the road itself lead you along. Just after you join a road coming from the left, **la Porta★** (72km ✝▲▲✖) comes into sight, adorning the crest of a declining ridge. The church campanile immediately steals your attention. This elegant, oriental-looking bell tower is supposedly the finest baroque tower on the island but, once alongside it, you discover that the 1720 structure has suffered a rather heavy-handed facelift. Park in the square and visit the church however: it's so seldom that one finds a church open on this island! The interior of St-Jean-Baptiste is lavishly decorated, with a beautifully-painted organ loft. Time for morning coffee? Find the *boulangérie*, buy some custard tarts and head over to the café, before you continue on through **Croce** (78km **M** of local customs, open Sat/Sun afternoons only). **Monte San Petrone★** (1767m/5795ft) is the most prominent upthrust in the area, with its rocky chest and crown.

Return to the D71 and bear left. This is the route of the drinking fountains: many are lovingly restored, and all are different. Art enthusiasts may like to summon up the energy to locate the key for the Church of St André in **Campana** (83km ✝) and then climb up to it. It holds a painting attributed to Zubarán or one of his pupils. Here Monte San Petrone rises up just beside you.

The Orezza Monastery (✝) is the impressive skeleton of a building you pass further on, draped in creepers. Once a seat for the Corsican Liberation Movement, this is where Paoli was elected Commander-in-Chief of the Corsican National Guard. It was destroyed in 1943. Further along you enter **Piedicroce** (87km ✝▲▲✖) and pass the massive church of St Peter and St Paul, overlooking the Orezza Valley. Its 17th-century organ is the oldest on Corsica, and the church also houses a 16th-century painting on wood of the Virgin and Child. A

urn-off left inside the village leads to the Orezza source
3.5km away; there is little to see, however).

Entering **Carcheto-Brustico★** (90.5km 🛉), a narrow
lane off left descends to the church of St Margaret,
where (if you can find the key) you would see two
works of local origin, an alabaster statuette and a painting of the Stations of the Cross in a Corsican setting.

The **Bocca d'Arcarota** (✕🖭) opens your way to the
vast Alesani Valley, flooded with trees. The sinuous
road describes a deep V, where the cloak of deciduous
trees fades out, and a tangle of maquis takes over. The
twisting tail of the Alesani Dam soon catches your eye
in the valley floor, with its cloudy-green water. An un-
marked lay-by (🖭) affords a good view over the dam.

Continuing the descent, your view stretches all along
the undulating sea plain. **Cervione** (121km 🛉🔺✕🖭M
🖭) is a balcony village, hooded by chestnuts and olive
trees. The imposing church here, St Mary and St Erasmus,
dwarfs even the tall houses that surround it. There is a
museum of local archaeology in the noticeably renovated Bishop's Palace (open daily except Sun/hol:
10.00-12.00; 14.30-18.00). Just beyond Cervione, visit
the chapel of Sta Cristina★ (🛉). Ask for the key at the
mairie/school in **Valle-di-Campoloro**, 0.5km outside
Cervione. Then turn left off the D71, down a country
lane, just beyond the mairie. Fork left again 1km down,
onto a dirt track signposted 'Santa Maria'. (Better still,
walk; the track is very bumpy.) The chapel holds exquisite 15th-century frescoes: the pastel colours are still
sharp, the facial expressions still very clearly defined.

From here return to the San Nicolao junction (D330)
and bear right. Pass through a tunnel and exit looking
straight up into a couple of small waterfalls that leap
down from a gap in the hillside. A path climbing above
the lay-by takes you to them. At this ideal picnic spot,
you'll find a shallow pool. Coming into **San Nicolao**
(127km 🛉🔺✕), a hillside village set in the shade of
trees, meet an intersection (🖭), from where you have a
fine view over a solitary 17th-century baroque church
with a six-storied campanile (🛉). Head right on the
D34; it leads to the N198/193 to Bastia.*

*A detour may be made on the homeward route: take the airport exit,
then bear right immediately on the D107, to visit La Canonica (🛉),
one of Corsica's finest churches (Romanesque, 12thC). The ancient
city of Mariana was founded here in 93BC. The 11th-century church
of San Parteo (🛉) is nearby. Continue to Bastia via the pretty lagoon.

Porto-Vecchio: THE OSPEDALE AND BAVELLA MASSIFS, AND A SUNSET OVER BONIFACIO

Porto-Vecchio • l'Ospedale • Zonza • Col de Bavella • Solenzara • Pinarellu • San Ciprianu • Porto-Vecchio • Plage de Palombaggia • Bonifacio • Porto-Vecchio

The roads in general are good but very winding. A stretch of 30km, however, between Argiavara and Solenzara, is very narrow and potholed. In bad weather the first part of the tour (as far as Solenzara) is not recommended due to poor visibility and the possibility of falling rocks and stones. Always be alert for foraging livestock. The high passes can be very cold with gale-force winds. Reckon on 214km/ 133mi; about 7h30min driving; leave Porto-Vecchio on the D368.

On route: **P** (see pages 11-14): 23, 24, 25; Walks 23, 24, 25

Ideally this drive should be a leisurely two-day affair so that you can fit in a couple of short, very spectacular walks, through some of the island's most impressive pink-granite mountains. But if you can't wait until tomorrow, make a mad dash to Bonifacio, to watch the sun set over the island's most dramatic town.

Setting out on the D368, head for Zonza, through countryside lightly wooded in the cork trees for which this region is well known. Their stripped trunks are a curious sight. A winding road leads you into the large, sprawling hills on the spine of the Ospedale Massif, which is home to a splendid forest of maritime pines. You enjoy stunning views over the deeply-etched Golfe de Porto-Vecchio and inland along the wide, open Stabiacco Valley that stretches back off the gulf. Bright green fields lining the valley floor stand out in this otherwise dark green countryside.

L'Ospedale (19km ✗🚗) takes its name from the hospital that was on this site in Roman times. It commands a magnificent panorama over the gulfs of Porto-Vecchio and Santa Manza. This small summer retreat with its granite-block mansions sits well camouflaged high on the wooded hillside amidst great boulders of granite.

Beyond the village you wind through the forest. Huge mounds of rock grow out of the cover of trees. You skirt the **Barrage de l'Ospedale**, a picturesque reservoir that lies at the foot of a prominent rock-faced hill. After crossing the dam wall, watch for the 'La Cascada' snack bar, on your right, 0.7km along. This is the starting point for Walk 24 to the **Cascade de Piscia di Gallo★** (**P**24), illustrated on page 124).

Cross the Bocca d'Illarata (991m/3250ft) and descend through forest into **Zonza** (40.5km ▲▲✗🚲).

Chestnut trees announce the beginning of this village. It sits at crossroads, deep in the hills. Here bear right on the D268 for the Col de Bavella. Back amidst trees again, you climb to the pass, with fine views across the valley onto bare, rocky ridges. Just over a small bridge (8km from Zonza) a lay-by allows you to pull over and safely enjoy the mountain scenery (📷).

Crossing the **Col de Bavella**★ (1218m/4000ft; 49km ▲✕📷*P*23; Walk 23) affords you one of Corsica's most breath-taking mountain vistas. The impenetrable valley walls with their thrusting crags (see photograph page 123) can be anything from a deep red to a soft rose colour. Seeing is believing! Large windswept pines stand here on the pass, as does a statue to Our Lady of the Snows. The hamlet of **Bavella** huddles just over the pass. A small gathering of stone, and wood and corrugated iron dwellings, it is more like a pastoral outpost than a hamlet. Descend in hairpin bends through a valley dominated by towering granite walls. Notice the flat-topped pines: this is not the lastest fashion in tree trimming; the strong winds are to blame. On the lower inclines you wend your way through plantations of firs, young pines, and chestnut trees. Closer to the valley floor, keep an eye open for a rocky outcrop that resembles a sitting dog (perhaps a terrier?). It sits atop a ridge on your left, about 15km down into the valley.

Once on the valley floor, you're in the company of the Solenzara River, a wide bouldery river bordered by beach-like stretches of sand. River swimmers will want to take a dip in its inviting pools, which are suitable for children. You meet the N198: turn right to pass through the sea-side town of **Solenzara** (80km ▲▲△✕🗨⊕) and follow the coast back to Porto-Vecchio. This stretch of coastline is flat and rocky, with a few pleasant beaches collaring the small bays. Fires have scarred much of the coastal hills. Pass behind the sweeping beaches of **Favone** (92km ▲▲▲△✕) and **Tarco** (96km ▲▲▲△✕). Curving round into an open bay, you spot a Genoese tower on a promontory, the Punta di Fautea (100km 🏠△✕).

Turning inland, the N198 soon enters **Ste-Lucie-de-Porto-Vecchio** (105km ▲▲✕🗨). Branch off left here onto the D168a, to see some of Porto-Vecchio's best-known beaches. Outside high season, **Pinarellu** (108km 🏠▲▲▲△✕🗨) is a quiet unassuming resort, sitting in a deep bay and guarded by a Genoese tower set on a tiny islet.. It boasts a fine beach bordered with pines. A pretty rural drive over a sometimes narrow and bumpy road leads you along the D468 to the next resort: some 8km from Pinarellu turn off left onto the D668. After 1km you come to a sweeping sandy beach, the **Plage de San Ciprianu** (118km ▲▲△✕⬛). If these first two beaches didn't take your fancy however, then try the next turn off to the left, the D468a, to the fine beach of **Cala Rossa** (▲▲▲△✕).

Continuing along the D468, you pass behind the very ritzy **Golfo di Sogno** (▲▲✕), which also offers good swimming in its sheltered bay. Returning to Porto-Vecchio, you're distracted by the prominent chain of inland mountains and the bay, across which sits the fortified town of Porto-Vecchio. As you approach, decide whether to call it a day or to make for Bonifacio.

At the roundabout you encounter on entering **Porto-Vecchio** (128km) bear left, following 'Port' and 'Centre Ville'. You pass the marina shown on page 24 and strike off right, soon rejoining the N198. Just 1km along, fork left on the Palombaggia road, to see the island's most highly-rated beach. Circling the estuary of the Stabiacco River, you look across the reedy tidal river with its pine-studded sand banks, to Porto-Vecchio (📷). A small pass takes you over the hills to **Picco-vagia**. From here you may wish to make an optional detour to the Pointe de la Chiappa (6km return; 📷▲). If so, take the first left in the hamlet, following signs for 'Village de Vacance la Chiappa'. Immediately into the turn-off, go left again on a bumpy dirt track to the lighthouses. From the top of the crest between the two lighthouses (military and civilian) you have an impressive view over the bays of San Ciprianu and Stagnolo, and onto the mountainous backdrop. On the left side of the point lie some rocky islets, the Iles Cerbicale.

The main tour continues straight through Piccovagia; after 1.5km, fork left for the **Plage de Palombaggia**★ (150km ▲▲▲△✕). This long unspoilt beach with its crystal-clear water, red rock, and low sand dunes is shaded by beautiful umbrella-shaped parasol pines. It would be easy just to lose the rest of the day here.

Return to the junction for the beach and bear left. More of this vast beach reveals itself through the trees along the shore. Sadly, the charred countryside and the new buildings do little to help conserve this very special stretch of coastline. At the village of **Bocca dell'**

Oro (160km ✕) keep right to rejoin the N198, where you bear left for Bonifacio.

Heading through low hills wooded in cork trees and maquis, you join the N196, which brings you into **Bonifacio★** (187km ✝🏠🏠▲△✕🏪WC🚐*P*25; Walk 25). For the citadel and old town, follow the Avenue Charles de Gaulle, to climb above the port. This magnificently-sited town, shown on page 127, overhangs the sea from its cliff-top perch. Set on a high, narrow headland, Bonifacio enjoys superb sea views on both sides. To the south it looks along the dramatic, glaring-white sea-cliffs, to the north down into the fiord-like inlet, and inland to the Cagna hills. Walk around the old town, inside the imposing and solid citadel walls. The elegant old buildings that line the narrow and shady streets are treasures of history. Visit the Eglise Sainte-Marie-Majeure, built by both the Pisans (in the late 12th century) and the Genoese. Its tall campanile dates back to the 14th and 15th centuries. The relics of St Boniface, the town's patron saint, are kept here, together with a piece of the 'True Cross'. Other churches of interest are St-François (1390) and St-Dominique, a Gothic church started in 1270 by the Knights Templar and finished by the Dominicans in 1343. The pillars of this latter church (between the aisles and the nave) have small paintings dating from the 18th century, representing the Fifteen Mysteries of the Rosary.

If you're spending the day at Bonifacio, among the more popular beaches are Calalonga, Rondinara, and those in the Golfe de Santa-Manza. Or you may want to take one of the boat trips on offer ... perhaps to the small granite Iles de Lavezzi, which boast a variety of unusual flora. Another popular excursion is to the sea caves, where you can see the famous 'King of Aragon's Staircase' with its 187 steps. Sardinia is also easily accessible from here. If you want to keep driving, visit the **Ermitage de la Trinité★**, 7km west of Bonifacio: head west towards Sartène and take the first left turn off the N196. This ancient sanctuary is the sight of a local pilgrimage, but it's best known for its striking view back onto Bonifacio. Finally, don't miss Walk 25. Of course you *can* reach the **Phare (lighthouse) de Pertusato★** by car, but you miss most of the dramatic coastline if you drive. Sunset is a fine time to end this walk, when the cliffs are aglow (see photograph page 128).

Then return to Porto-Vecchio (214km).

❀ Walking

This book features walks over most of Corsica, with particular emphasis on the north and west. The walks have been chosen for their accessibility from the centres most popular with holidaymakers and cover a good cross-section of the island's unique and varied landscapes. Because there are books available on mountain climbing (including the well-known 'Topo Guides'), I have concentrated on less strenuous routes, especially walks that can be completed in a day's outing from your overnight base. There are walks for all the family, rambles accessible to hill walkers of all ages, and the inevitable (given the terrain) 'huffing and puffing' hikes for the very fit. All the walks are graded.

The Parc Régional de la Corse has done a lot of waymarking on the island and set up many excellent trails. Of these, the best known is the GR20. More recent and much less strenuous trails are the 'Tra Mare e Monti' ('Sea and Mountains') footpath from Calenzana to Cargése; the 'Mare a Mare' ('Sea to Sea') path from Alzu to Propriano, and another route from Acquacitosa to Cruciata. All are dotted with refuges. They are also developing various 'Sentiers de Pays', local walks based on centres like Venaco: for information about these, enquire at the Regional Park Headquarters mentioned below under 'Maps'. All routes are well waymarked. I have included some sections of the 'Sea and Mountains' path and some Sentiers de Pays, as well as easier stretches of the GR20 in this book.

Maps and guides

You will find the **maps** in this book sufficient for any one-day walks you tackle on Corsica. Should you wish to go further afield, see notes about maps on page 6.

Quite a bit of printed material (in French) is to be found once you are on the island, at bookshops and in the local tourist information offices (*syndicats d'initiative*). You can also contact the headquarters of the Parc Régional de la Corse (4 Rue Fiorella, Ajaccio; tel: 95.21.56.54). They will be happy to provide leaflets or give you the names of **guides** covering the mountain routes in the area you wish to explore.

Where to stay

The walks have been written up from four bases: Ajaccio/Porto, Calvi, Bastia and Porto-Vecchio. Not only are these the most popular tourist areas at present, but they are also quite well served by public transport. Ajaccio and Calvi are the largest tourist areas in the north, and provide all the usual requirements for holidaymaking. Bastia, which is much less 'touristy', is nevertheless popular with many visitors. Porto-Vecchio is the main base in the south of the island.

The independent traveller will find that there are hotels, apartments, *pensions* and camping grounds in most corners of the island. However many are only open from June 15th to September 15th. *Note:* In July and August nearly all the accommodation is booked — some of it months in advance. During June and September, reserving a couple of days in advance is usually sufficient, but not in the peak months! The rates for accommodation outside July and August are also far more reasonable than in high season. Never be afraid to ask for a discount out of season.

Gîtes (de France), country cottages, are also widely scattered across the island. These are usually rented by the month, however. Write to the French Tourist Office for further information: ask for the booklet 'Gîtes de France — Corse'. *Gîtes d'etape* are different. They are more akin to youth hostels. Some are manned, others not; occasionally meals are provided. They are geared for outdoor/sports people.

Refuges are found liberally dotted around the central mountains. Part of the GR20/Mare e Monti/Mare a Mare programme, they are well maintained, open all year round, and fully equipped (gas, kitchen utensils, beds, etc).

Weather

Mid-June until mid-September is most reliable for walking on Corsica — and the best for swimming, too. On either side of this 'high season', the weather can be changeable, which means that some of the mountain walks can be extremely dangerous. Snow may lie as low as 1000m/3300ft in June and may fall again late in September.

In **May** and **October** you will usually encounter more good days than bad ones, but be sure of the weather before setting off for the mountains. Cloud or mist sometimes descend without warning, and the temperatures fall rapidly. May and October are best suited for walks below the mountains. The weather, even if it turns bad, is not usually bad enough to ruin an entire day ... although it can get very cold. These are, however, the months of the flowers and autumnal colours in the forests. In spring the countryside will be scented with the strong perfume of the maquis; in autumn the beech and the chestnut groves are an extravaganza of yellows and golds, and the shepherds return with their flocks — a wonderful sight.

July and **August** are the really hot months, when temperatures often climb into the 30s. Things to fear are dehydration, the frightening electrical storms and forest fires. *Always carry plenty of water*, as many mountain streams dry up in the summer, and *guard against the sun*. **Electrical storms** usually come with plenty of warning: seek shelter away from exposed places.

As a general rule, the north of Corsica is hotter than the south, and the east is wetter than the west. And the place which boasts the most sunshine (in the whole of France) is Ajaccio.

Wind patterns on the island make for quite a study! Here are some names you might hear or see in the newspapers:

The *libeccio:* a strong wind from the southwest, hot and dry in summer; in winter it carries rain to the west;

The *maestral:* the Corsican version of the *mistral,* this wind comes from the northwest and is unpleasant all year round, with a whining violence. Fortunately, it blows infrequently;

The *sirocco:* a dry dusty wind from the southeast;

The *grecale:* blowing from the northeast, it carries rain to the north, but leaves the south unaffected;

The *tramontane:* a dry cold wind from the north, it blows very infrequently, but is strong enough to knock you off your feet;

The *mezzogiorno:* the 'midday' wind — caused by the interaction of the hot sun and the still-cold sea, which raises strong sea breezes along the coast.

Finally, it cannot be stressed too strongly that **one must always be fully equipped for all extremes of weather**. Every year deaths are reported, and these are invariably caused through lack of caution. *Do* read the important note on page 2 and the country code on page 136 *carefully.*

What to take

If you're already on Corsica when you find this book, and you haven't any special equipment such as a rucksack or walking boots, you can still do many of the walks — or you can buy the basic equipment at one of the sports shops catering for walkers and climbers. *Don't* attempt the more difficult walks without the proper gear. For each walk in the book, the *minimum* year-round equipment is listed. Above all, you need stout, thick-soled shoes or walking boots. *Ankle support* is always advisable and is *essential* on some of the walks, where the path descends steeply over loose stones. You may find the following checklist useful:

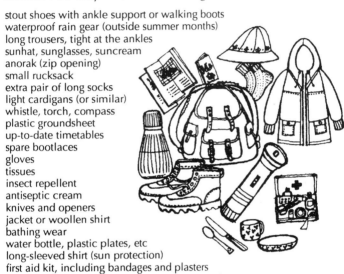

stout shoes with ankle support or walking boots
waterproof rain gear (outside summer months)
long trousers, tight at the ankles
sunhat, sunglasses, suncream
anorak (zip opening)
small rucksack
extra pair of long socks
light cardigans (or similar)
whistle, torch, compass
plastic groundsheet
up-to-date timetables
spare bootlaces
gloves
tissues
insect repellent
antiseptic cream
knives and openers
jacket or woollen shirt
bathing wear
water bottle, plastic plates, etc
long-sleeved shirt (sun protection)
first aid kit, including bandages and plasters
'Dog Dazer' (see 'Things that bite ...', page 56)

Language

Corse — in all its many dialects — is the language spoken on the island. French is, however, spoken in all the tourist areas. Should you get off the beaten track and have to ask directions, you should be able to make yourself understood with some French or Italian, even in the mountains.

There's a very strong interest in using Corsican spelling for place names. I have tried to use the spellings I found on signposts in all the tour and walk descriptions, but even these vary when referring to the same place!

You will spot inconsistencies in the text, on maps, and on local signposts; unfortunately, this is unavoidable.

Try to learn a few words of greeting and thanks in Corse; they'll go down a treat with the local people.

Things that bite, sting, or shoot

Dogs are not generally a problem on Corsica, since most of the time you'll be far from habitation. In summer, however, some of the shepherds' dogs may send shivers down your spine. Let the shepherd know you're around, and you won't have any worries. Lone country houses always have a guard dog ... or three. Watch their tails and heed their barks and growls. If you're worried, wait for the owner to emerge before you continue. You may like to invest in an ultrasonic 'Dog Dazer': for information, write to Dazer UK, 51 Alfriston Road, London SW11 6NR. In the walking notes I always warn of unfriendly dogs on the route.

The **shooting season** for all game is from the third Sunday in August until the first Sunday in January. Some bird-shooting extends until the end of March. It can be very unnerving to have hunters blasting away all around you! If you fear they are too close, don't be afraid to bellow out — in *any* language!

You'll be pleased to read that while **snakes** and **insects** are to be found on the island, none has a fatal bite or sting.

Organisation of the walks

The twenty-five main walks in this book are written up from the four main tourist centres: Ajaccio/Porto (Walks 1-11), Calvi (Walks 12-18), Bastia (Walks 19-22) and Porto-Vecchio (Walks 23-25).

I hope that the book is set out so that you can plan your walks easily — depending on how far you want to go, your abilities and equipment ... and what time you are willing to get up in the morning! You might begin by considering the fold-out touring map between pages 16 and 17. Here you can see at a glance the overall terrain, the road and rail network, and the general orientation of the walking maps in the text.

Quickly flipping through the book, you'll find that there is at least one photograph for every walk. Having selected one or two potential excursions from the map and the photographs, look over the planning information at the beginning of the walks. Here you'll find distance/walking time, grade, equipment, and how to get there by public transport. If the walk appears to be beyond your fitness or ability, check to see if a short or alternative version is described, which *would* appeal to you. On very hot days, the picnic strolls and short walk suggestions on pages 11-14 may be as strenuous an adventure as you'd like to tackle.

When you are on your walk, you will find that the text begins with an introduction to the overall land-scape and then quickly turns to a detailed description of the route itself. The large-scale walking maps (all reproduced from IGN maps, scale 1:50,000) have been specially annotated to show key landmarks and, where possible, set out facing the walking notes. Times are given for reaching certain points in the walk. I have tried to estimate these times for the average, reasonably fit walker. So if you're a beginner, or if you prefer a leisurely pace, a walk may take you **much longer**. Don't forget to take transport connections at the end of the walk into account! The most important factor is *consistency* of walking times, and I suggest that you compare your times with mine on one or two short walks, before you embark on a long hike.

Below is a **key to the symbols** used on the maps:

	Tarred roads: four lanes; two lanes
	Tarred roads: three lanes; narrow
	Narrow roads: regularly surfaced; irregularly surfaced
	Forestry track, etc. Logging track or footpath
	Old cart track. Road under construction.
	Railways: two tracks, one track; electrified line; station; stop
PF SP	Boundaries: administrative centre; district
	Boundaries: military camp; firing range
	Boundaries: state forest; national park; outer limits
	Source. Well. Water tower. Reservoir. Bridge; footbridge
	Church. Chapel, shrine. Cross, religious statue. Cemetery
Tr Tr Chem.	Tower. Dungeon. Windmill. Wind-pump. Chimney
	Triangulation point. Blast furnace. Pylon. Quarry
Mon.	Bus stop. Car parking. Monument. Château. Ruins
	Dolmen, menhir. Viewpoint, best views. Camping
	Hall, hangar. Fort. Casemate.
Mine Cave P	Mine. Cave. Refuge. Picnic spot. Picnic tables
	Route of walk. Alternative route
	Contour lines, 20 m intervals. Hollow. Basin. Scree

1 POINTE DE LA PARATA • ANSE DE MINACCIA • POINTE DE LA PARATA

Distance/time: 16.5km/10.3mi; 4h50min

Grade: easy, but some thorny scrub on route. No shade on beaches, can be very hot. An ascent of 100m/330ft.

Equipment: light shoes, sunhat, sunglasses, suncream, long-sleeved shirt, raingear, swimwear, picnic, water

How to get there: 🚌 to the Pointe de la Parata (Timetable 1)
To return: same bus

Short walk: Pointe de la Parata — Capigliolo — Anse de Minaccia — Capigliolo — Capigliolo turn-off: easy, but a steady 35-minute ascent up a dirt road beyond Capigliolo. 2h45min. Follow the main walk to the Anse de Minaccia. Then return to Capigliolo and take the dirt road out of this hamlet (keeping straight on). At the D111b, turn right for Ajaccio Bay and your bus.

This walk is an excellent 'starter' and puts you into the holiday mood straight away. It's easy, gives you a taste of the beaches to come, and takes you through picturesque countryside. In spring you'll be intoxicated by the sweet-smelling maquis, when the hillsides are ablaze with a riot of brightly-coloured flowers.

The turquoise sea from the maquis-covered cliffs, not far beyond the setting for Picnic 1.

Take the town bus to the end of the line, the Pointe de la Parata. This rocky promontory is the site of a 17th-century Genoese tower, built as a defence against the Moors. Beyond the point lie the Iles Sanguinaires, a group of sharp granite islets. As all the guide books point out, they are best seen under the setting sun, when they give off a pinkish glow. (An easy, 20-minute stroll round the point would give you a closer look.)

Setting off on the main walk, take the path alongside the restaurant, where a small plaque with a map marks the beginning of the route. Following the wide gravelly path, you're immediately swallowed up in maquis, a low mat of Mediterranean scrub. An array of spring flowers holds your attention all along, and yellow spiny broom lights up the hillsides. You head round into a aquamarine-coloured bay, set at the foot of dark green hills. Vivid carmine *Lampranthus* covers the banks. In about **7min** come to a rifle range; skirt it to the right, through the *Lampranthus*. Meet a faint track and follow it uphill. Soon pass through a fence and come to a larger track; head left here. A few minutes along, notice the pink-and-yellow-coloured rock on the hillock over to the left. In **25min** you're crossing a low crest. Over the crest, you look down into a small rocky cove (**P1**). The track descends to it, but you bear right, along the wide path. Lizards galore dart across your path, as you brush your way through flowers.

At around **55min** a superb view greets you, as you cross over a ridge. Two beautiful beaches rest in the now-flat coastline: the first is small and circular, the second large and sweeping. The white sand glares in the sunlight. An open grassy valley, sheltered by high rocky hills, empties out into the bay. The arm of the cape rolls gently out to the left. Descending, you soon come to a track above the first cove, to find the little holiday hamlet of Capigliolo. Immediately beyond the house below the track, scramble down the steep rocky slope and onto the beach, the Plage de St-Antoine.

At the end of this blinding-white cove, squeeze through the rocks and mount the bank to continue along the shore. Just beyond the next cove, a clearer path leads you to the Anse (Cove) de Minaccia. The countryside is completely unspoiled. Cows graze in the fields, and nudists loaf on the beach. I'll bet I know which gets your attention first! Cross the fence and slide down onto the beach (**1h20min**). Twenty minutes along, a fence blocks the way. At low tide you can round the end of it, otherwise crawl under the railing (this allows people through, but not the cows).

Continue beyond the fence around the rocky shore-line, remaining on the rocks. Pass a small cove seven minutes along. You'll see the occasional blue dot and arrow on the rock but, generally, no one ventures this far. A little under 20 minutes from the fence you pass below a fenced-off field. Just beyond it, pick up a path that heads around the hillside, just above the rocky shore line (a very short stretch of this path may be unnerving for the inexperienced hiker, but the way is generally easy going). Pass behind an inviting sandy beach less than 15 minutes from the fenced-off field. Or, you can cross the beach and pick up your path at the other end of it. A beach hut sits off the shore here.

At **2h25min**, a little over five minutes from the last cove, you reach yet another striking cove — the last. Scramble over the fence or go through the gate to reach it. Return the same way, or take the Short walk route beyond Capigliolo (**4h50min**).

Walk 2: On the climb from the Col de Listincone to Appietto, the Rocher des Gozzi, your goal, stands out above the vivid green squares of cultivation and dark hillocks of the Gravona Valley.

2 LISTINCONE • APPIETTO • ROCHER DES GOZZI • LISTINCONE

Distance/time: 11km/7mi; 3h20min   **See photograph opposite**

Grade: moderate to strenuous; an ascent of 485m/1590ft. The (somewhat overgrown) path is slippery when wet. The rock itself is vertiginous and potentially dangerous.

Equipment: sturdy shoes or walking boots, sunhat, sunglasses, suncream, long-sleeved shirt, long trousers, cardigan, anorak, raingear, picnic, water

How to get there: 🚌 to the Col de Listincone (Timetables 2, 3)
To return: same buses

The Rocher des Gozzi is the most noticeable landmark in the Gravona Valley northeast of Ajaccio. Every time you leave the town, there it stands — a solid mass of bare rock rising straight up off the plains. The best time to end this walk is in the evening, when the soft rose colour of the rock intensifies under the fading light. The stupendous panorama from the summit is ample reward for the climb the walk entails.

The bus drops you at the Col (Pass) de Listincone, the turn-off for Appietto. **Start out** by following the road up towards the village, part of which soon appears high on the hillside above. From here the Rocher de Gozzi is a sheer buttress of rock with a thimble-shaped hat at its summit (see photograph opposite). About **35min** up (some 50m/yds before the village cemetery), turn off onto a dirt track striking off right and follow it over to the Chapel of San Chirgu on the ridge opposite. From here you have a fine view of Appietto, a village dating from the Middle Ages, once the home of the Counts of Cinarca. It consists of three separate hamlets: the highest, with its miniature castle, and the lowest, with its lovely mansions, are the more picturesque.

Pick up your path at the end of the track, just beside some sort of measuring apparatus (or so I guess it to be). A goats' trail now leads you up the spine of the ridge. Soon clamber over a fence on a rickety stile of sorts. (The sign here, 'Private Property; it is an offence to enter', can be safely ignored, since you have right of way to the ancient castle site.) Keep straight up the crest of the ridge, brushing your way through the maquis. The hills fold back, and the vast Golfe d'Ajaccio comes into view. Tiny pink butterfly orchids shelter amidst the *Cistus* and *Asphodelus*. On your right you look down onto a clean, unsettled valley ensconced in the hills running up from Lava Bay. The Punta Pozzo di Borgo is the highest of these hills, and the lonely conspicuous

Château de la Punta is perched on its slopes. It belongs to the Pozzo di Borgo family, descendents of Charles André Pozzo di Borgo, Napoleon's great enemy.

Cutting through the dense flora, your way splinters and rejoins: remain on the crest. At around **55min**, you'll find yourself fenced in. A large rock enables you (once you've scrambled up it) to step over the fence. Several minutes later, pass through a collapsed stone wall that runs straight down the spine of the ridge. Now you're on its right-hand flanks, and a rock 'balcony' serves as as excellent viewing point minutes later.

Attention is needed at around **1h10min**. Your path branches off to the right and heads around the hillside towards the Rocher des Gozzi which, from this vantage point, looks about eye-level. No obvious landmarks are here to alert you, so look out for a faint path crossing the ridge here and joining the one you are on. At this point you are in a small clearing and just below a hilltop. Continue along this goats' trail (a short strip of path a minute along might prove unnerving for inexperienced walkers). You round a fold in the slope and look straight across to the impressive rock … and Ajaccio.

The path divides once in a while, so stay on an even contour, following either path. The hillside drops off into a precipitous wall down to the plain below. At about **1h40min** you're alongside the derelict stone building that you glimpsed from your earlier viewpoint. The Rocher des Gozzi sits directly behind it. A few minutes across, scramble down into a gap slicing across the neck of the rock. Ravines now fall away on either side of you. Notice also the pinnacle of rock bursting up on your right. All fours are needed, if you really want to explore. It's vertiginous from here on! Scant remains of stone walls appear (**1h50min**) — part of a medieval château that once belonged to the Counts of Cinarca. And what a view you have: you 'hang' straight out over the Gravona Plain and look towards the gulf.

Watch the swifts swooping in and out and the lizards hunting, before you return to Listincone the same way (**3h20min**). Flag down the bus where you left it.

3 COL ST-GEORGES • PIETROSELLA • CRUCIATA

Distance/time: 19km/12mi; 6h15min

Grade: easy but long, with an initial climb of about 85m/280ft

Equipment: sturdy shoes or boots, sunhat, sunglasses, suncream, long-sleeved shirt, long trousers, cardigan, raingear, picnic, water

How to get there: 🚍 to the Col St-Georges (Timetable 4)

To return: 🚍 from the Cruciata turn-off to Ajaccio (Timetable 6)

Alternative walk: Col St-Georges — Buselica — Porticcio: grade as above; 6h05min. Follow the main walk up to the Pietrosella/Porticcio junction (1h40min), where the main walk goes left. Turn right; your route is waymarked with orange paint. Almost immediately the track ends; continue on a path. Keep right at a fork 15min along and, 25min later (2h20min), ignore a faint fork off to the right. At 3h meet a fork and keep left. Soon reach the D302. Follow it downhill to the right for 40min, then fork left, on a driveway signposted for Porticcio. Metres/yards up this driveway, turn right on a track. It soon narrows into a path. Some 4h10min along leave the scrub and keep straight ahead across a field. You meet a small road: climb it for 8mins, then turn left down a driveway (opposite a house with yappy dogs). Turn left again on a path flanked by fences and exit through a gate. Minutes later, without warning, the path veers off left. At a junction (Liscinosa; 5h), head uphill left. Eight minutes later, go left again, at another T-junction. Meet a confusing junction of four paths 3min later, where a sign on a tree indicates Porticcio, straight on (the right-hand fork). Follow the sign. There's no more waymarking beyond this point. You reach the road 15min from the junction; bear right and, metres/yards along, take the path descending to the left. Keep left at a fork and soon come out at the back of an equestrian centre. Skirt the right-hand side of it, quietly, and leave it by the track. Turn left along the D555 and, at the roundabout, keep right for Porticcio (6h05min). The bus stop is to the right (Timetable 6). It's possible to walk along this superb beach all the way to the airport (1h15min), but make sure that the lagoon outlet *is shallow and not fast-flowing* before you cross it. Catch one of the frequent city buses to Ajaccio behind the beach.

Here's a taste of the little hills … to get you into training for the real ones! Winding your way along the crests of ridges, you disappear into woods of maquis, surfacing now and again for a view of snow-capped peaks and the immense Ajaccio Gulf. And in the autumn you

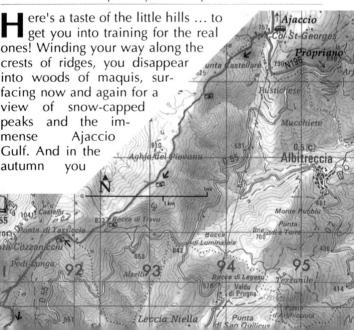

can eat the fruit (strawberries, believe it or not), off the *Arbutus* trees till it's coming out of your ears.

Start the walk at the Auberge Col St-Georges. Dashes of orange paint lead you to your destination. Walk up the tarred lane on the left-hand side of the inn. This gives way to a gravel track, then a path flanked by kermes and holly oak trees. At **8min** cross a stream and bear right. Almost at once, come to a fork: bear left uphill. A short ascent follows, to a crest from where you'll enjoy sweeping views over the wooded hills and tiny villages set like islands in a sea of maquis.

Some **35min** into the walk you emerge onto a windy plateau overgrown with strawberry trees and heather. In a couple of minutes, come to a fork and bear right

through a clump of alder trees. Pass through a gate, and shortly reach the end of a track. Keep left. Not far off **50min** you cross the ridge and look out over the deep blue Ajaccio Gulf. The Plage de Porticcio (Alternative walk, photograph page 66) is the long collar of white sand that lights it up. Ajaccio stands out clearly, resting up against the hills of the Punta di Lisa.

Approaching **1h05min** pass through a stone wall with a chain barrier at the Bocca di Travu. Some 18m/yds beyond the wall take the clear path forking off to the right (waymarked). You enter a dense wood of maquis and kermes oak. In autumn the ground is littered with pale pink cyclamen. The freshly-dug patches of earth are a sign that wild pigs are about.

The way widens into a track and climbs to a junction (**1h40min**). Bear left for Pietrosella and Bisinao, as

signposted. (The Alternative walk heads right here, for Porticcio.) A rough gravel track takes you down to the D55, at a junction. Cross the D302 and pick up your path (really an overgrown track) behind the road signs. Eight minutes along the path, fork off right onto another path. Waymarking on a rock just inside the path reassures you. This moss-laden path leads you through a tangle of trees. Heading along the valley floor you pass 'islands' of fields, buried amidst the mat of vegetation that covers the inclines. A babbling brook runs down the valley floor just below you.

At **3h25min** cross a country road and continue straight on for Pietrosella. Fifteen minutes later the path joins a small lane, just below the village. Minutes up the lane, you're in Pietrosella. This little village slumbers in a quiet, out-of-the-way valley. Were you to turn left now along the D255a, in three minutes you would come to a path on your right to the shady village washing place and a fountain (but the water is not drinkable). It makes a good place to stop for lunch.

The main walk turns right on the D255a. After 100m/yds you'll see a sign for Cruciata. Head up the driveway that circles the village church, ascending the hillside behind it. Pass a couple of secluded

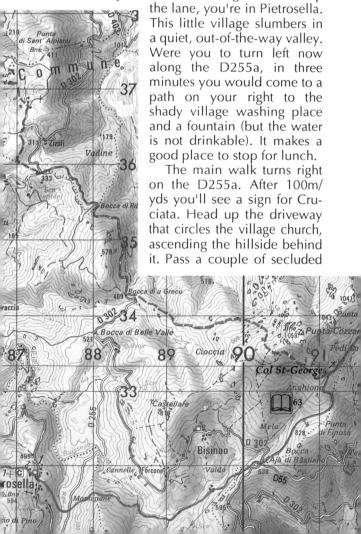

The Plage de Porticcio. You'll often see birds in the lovely lagoon.

houses (mind the guard dog here). When the driveway ends, follow the path heading off it and, minutes along keep right at a fork. Piece by piece the magnificent Golfe d'Ajaccio unfolds. You look out over maquis-clad hills to the wooded fingers of land that reach out into the bay. Sweeping, sandy bays separate these fingers. Ajaccio sits across the still waters at the foot of bare rocky, hills.

At **5h25min** you pass a fork off to the right, as you head along the top of the crest. Less than 25 minutes later, you leave the path (beside a cemetery), to continue downhill on a dirt track. Coming into the small hillside settlement of Cruciata the way becomes tarred; keep right at a fork. At about **6h15min** you reach the Porticcio road. The bus stop lies along to your right.

4 VERGHIA • FORET DOMANIALE DE CHIAVARI • LE RUPPIONE

Distance/time: 17km/10.5mi; 5h   **See map opposite**

Grade: moderate climb of 475m/1560ft on a forestry track

Equipment: sturdy shoes, sunhat, sunglasses, suncream, long-sleeved shirt, warm cardigan, raingear, swimwear, picnic, water

How to get there: 🚌 to Verghia (Timetable 6)
To return: same bus from le Ruppione

Short walk: Verghia — hillside circuit — Verghia: easy, equipment/ access as above; 1h25min. Follow the main walk for 15min, then turn left at the junction. Follow the track-cum-path here for 40min, until it ends. Just before this track narrows into a hedged-in path, turn left down another path, cross a streambed and then climb to a track. Turn left downhill on the track, ignoring a faint track forking off left. Soon meet a gravel road cutting across in front of you (1h05min): bear left along it. In 8min reach the D55. Minutes along to the left you're back at the track where you entered the forest, 10min from the bus stop.

This walk takes you through a magnificent forest of cork trees, kermes and holm oaks, eucalyptus and maquis, to the shell of an enormous stately building that towers above the treetops.

Take the bus to the end of the line, then walk back along the bus route for 10 minutes, to the turn-off to the Forêt Dominiale de Chiavari (written on a rock on the left-hand side of the track). **Start the walk** by turning right onto the forestry track and head up into the old crusty-trunked trees. Ignore the first fork off to the right, and you'll come to a junction within **15min**. The main walk turns right here. The Short walk (which is *strongly recommended for everyone,* especially in springtime), heads left. Birds galore accompany you, whichever flower-splashed route you choose (**P4**).

Close on **35min** pass a small fenced-in graveyard on the right. Continue straight on at the junction a couple of minutes later. Approaching the road, the track widens into a grand avenue bordered with eucalytus trees and, in **1h**, you come to the road. Return to the forest along the track just above you, heading back in the direction you've just come. In a few minutes come to a junction: bear left and pass through a barrier. Glimpses of Ajaccio and the gulf may be caught through the trees now and again. Then, at **1h30min**, a break in the vegetation offers superb views over the Anse Ottioni, the bay where you set out. The Punta di Sette Nave is the headland jutting out into the gulf, adorned by the Genoese Tour de l'Isolella.

You swing back into a large, open valley, and the stately ruin (Laticapso on the map) catches your eye, hidden in the trees. Shortly after passing a turning left you come to this mysterious building (**2h30min**), shown below. Behind it, your continuing route forks: descend to the left. Pass a drinking fountain, just a trickle, set in a stone wall. Go left again at the next fork. The track narrows as you descend towards the coast, soon enjoying views over the white-collared Anse Ottioni and more coves to the south. Flowers reappear alongside the track: the scent of spiny broom is particularly strong. As you leave the valley you've just circled you'll overlook the harbour again, across to Ajaccio and the hazy hills in the background. Pretty rocky coves, bitten out of the coastline below, capture your attention with their brightness. Across from you, taking advantage of this view, is the settlement of Acelasca.

At **4h** you leave through a barrier and come to an intersection. Keep straight on, rounding the hillside. You'll catch sight of a combe lined with fields not far below, then you're hedged in by trees again. Soon you're passing through a wood of tall, thin eucalyptus trees; they creak and groan in the wind. Ignore the faint fork off to the right, beyond which the track splits and rejoins, and then another faint fork, this one on the left.

Approaching **4h20min** come to a junction and bear left, down a wider track, under trees intertwined with vines and creepers. You leave the valley soaking up the scent of lavender and broom, to meet the D55 (**5h**) and hear the waves crashing on the shore. A lovely beach is just opposite. The bus stop is up to your right, just outside the police station (*gendarmerie*) at le Ruppione.

At 2h30min you come upon the shell of a once-great edifice, in a glade edged with planes and elms. Perfectly symmetrical, it stands proud, even in its derelict state. It gives no hint of its past, but holds the air of a sanctuary.

5 LA FOCE • CASCADES DES ANGLAIS • L'ANCIEN REFUGE DU CAF • VIZZAVONA

See map on reverse of touring map
Distance/time: 8.5km/5.3mi; 4h10min
Grade: moderate-strenuous, with some short steep scrambles. Ascent of 450m/1475ft. Can be very cold. Recommended for good weather only; dangerous when wet.
Equipment: walking boots, sunhat, sunglasses, suncream, long-sleeved shirt, long trousers, cardigan, anorak, gloves, raingear, wimwear, picnic, water
How to get there: 🚌 to la Foce (near Vizzavona; Timetable 7)
To return: 🚂 from Vizzavona (Timetable 21), or 🚌 (Timetable 7)

The cascading Agnone River is the essence of this walk. It bounds down a valley of rock into deep emerald-green pools. Monte d'Oro (2389m/7835ft), Corsica's fifth highest peak, dominates the valley. An apron of pines stretches around its lower slopes, but the valley itself is the home of a splendid beech forest. Of all these beautiful gifts of nature, it's the river you'll remember ... and the dazzling Cascades des Anglais.

La Foce is just over the Vizzavona Pass (Col), so get ready to leave the bus as soon as you cross it. **Start off** just downhill (north) from the handful of houses that make up la Foce: turn left onto a forestry track and into the beech trees. Monte d'Oro soon appears through the trees, filling in this picture. Its naked rocky crown rises high above the pine wood patching its inclines.

Less than **15min** along, the track swings down to the right, but you keep straight on to the crystal-clear, bubbly river, with its green and alluring pools. Here you meet the GR20 (**25min**; *P*5). At the end of the walk, you will cross the bridge and follow the GR20 into Vizzavona but, for now, follow it *uphill*, remaining on the left-hand side of the river. The Agnone bounces down the valley alongside you, one falls after another (he 'Cascades des Anglais'). There is no clearly-trodden path, so follow the red and white waymarking.

The route is very steep at times; sometimes you'll be using all fours. In just under **1h** cross a side-stream. Green lichen illuminates the surrounding rock; under direct sunlight it glows with the fluorescence of a highlighter pen. At **1h25min** ignore a turn-off to the left, then cross the river on the footbridge shown on page 70, above a small but thundering waterfall. When you come to the remains of the old French Alpine Club (CAF) refuge at **1h40min**, the spring snow-line is not far out of reach. Just below this small crumbled rock shelter is the

69

largest waterfall in the valley. You're completely en-
circled by mountains. In the hills behind la Foce, the
Monte Renoso chain may still be wearing a mantle of
snow (see cover photograph).

The walk ends here at the refuge. (If you have time,
you might like to continue on the GR20, or climb
Monte d'Oro to a viewpoint over the tiny, hidden Lac
d'Oro. These paths are shown on the map, but are
recommended for experienced walkers only. Be sure to
leave time to get back for the last train from Vizzavona.)

Heading back, don't miss the beryl-green pools that
lie concealed in the valley floor; some are magnificent.
But if you decide to swim in the Agnone, make sure the
pools are safe before you hurl yourself into them; the
current can be very strong indeed. Return to the Vizzavona turn-off (1h25min back; **3h05min**), then turn left
to cross the bridge. For a short time you follow an old
cobbled path. Some 25min beyond the bridge, cross a
small wooden bridge and come to a track, where you
head downhill to the right. Some minutes later cross a
track; a junction follows: head downhill to the right.
Come to another junction 100m/yds along and this time
swing left. In a further eight minutes (just 20 paces
before a concrete bridge), fork right on a path, heading
into the trees. A little wooden bridge lies ahead, and a
dot of yellow paint indicates the way. Go left at the first
junction (in 3min) and cross a second little bridge.

The beech-shaded path brings you into the back of
Vizzavona, a tranquil hamlet of villas, inns and res-
taurants (**4h10min**). The railway station is not far
downhill to the left. (The main road/bus stop is ten
minutes uphill to the right.)

*Left: Wooden bridge over the Agnone,
above the Cascades des Anglais (Walk
5). Right and far right: The Bergerie de
Tolla, from a book of fairy tales. Small
stone dwellings sit in a sheltered grassy
clearing in the middle of the woods.
High rocky crags lean back out of the
valley walls. Watch out for the three
cute, but very mischievous donkeys
here. They wander over to greet you full
of innocence, and just as you try to slip
past they reach for a nibble of your ...
you know what!*

See map on reverse of touring map; see also photograph page 20

Distance/time: 16km/10mi; 5h10min

Grade: moderate, with a long climb of 290m/950ft. Highly recommended for any fit walker, but not advisable in bad weather.

Equipment: sturdy shoes or walking boots, sunhat, sunglasses, suncream, swimwear, long trousers, long-sleeved shirt, gloves, cardigan, warm jacket, rainwear, picnic, water

How to get there: ☒ to Tattone (Timetable 21)
To return: same train

I first did this walk in autumn, and what a splendour awaited me. The beech trees left me in awe with their golds and yellows. The streams and rivers were magnificent cascades, filled by the autumn rains. Deep in the valley a wisp of smoke curling above the trees lead me to the Bergerie de Tolla, a lonely pastoral outpost. Entering it was like walking into a children's story book.

The walk starts straight off the station platform at Tattone. Head off along the railway tracks in the direction of Corte. Some 140m/yds along, cross the tracks and follow the path that disappears into the pines. Out of the trees you come onto a small country road. Turn left along it for Canaglia, less than an hour away. This small hamlet (**1h**) sits high on a hillside between the pine forest and chestnut trees, overlooking the confluence of the Manganello and the Vecchio rivers.

In two minutes we're through the hamlet and continuing on the signposted forestry track that heads up into the valley. High rocky summits peer above the thickly-wooded walls. You pass a couple of pig-pens; their smell gives them away long before you see them. A good **1h05min** into the walk the track forks. Dashes

of orange paint lead you down to the right. Pass a faint fork off to the right and come to the narrow, thundering Manganello River (**1h25min**). (If you plan to swim, take the strong current into account.) The way narrows here, and alders grow along the riverside.

Close on **2h20min** you round a corner, to see a waterfall crashing down at the edge of the path (see photograph page 20), and a bridge takes you over its cascading waters. The higher you climb the more striking the colours become, especially in the beech forest up ahead. A few minutes above the waterfall, leave this path and cross the Manganello, following a signpost for the Bergerie de Tolla. (However, on your return from the *bergerie*, provided you're not all puffed out, I do recommend wandering up the path to the left signposted to the Refuge de l'Onda, for about thirty-five minutes. In autumn it's a must! You'll soon find yourself in a dense wood where moss coats the trees and drips off the rocks. It could be a Japanese garden. Don't forget though to add your time on to the walk times.)

The Grottacia River joins the Manganello just where you cross it. Once again you'll be reaching for your camera, to capture the Manganello on film, as it surges out of a rocky gorge leaving swirling beryl-green pools in its wake. Once over the river, your waymarking changes to the red and white stripes of the GR20. The livestock have created their own trails here, so be sure to follow the waymarked route. The path curves into a side valley on the right. Don't forget to look behind you: high on the mountainside you'll spot a beech wood, a spectacular fire of colours in autumn.

Heading through a gap in the hills you enter an enclosed valley and stumble upon the 'story book' Bergerie de Tolla, shown on page 71 (**2h35min**). For most of you this will be far enough. However, even more spectacular scenery lies further up the valley. (You could continue for another 50 minutes, or until you reach a log bridge crossing the river to your left, from where you look straight up into a cascade that leaps and bounds down the valley wall. To get there, take the path to the right of the last house at the *bergerie*, passing the mischievous donkeys shown on page 71.)

Your return to Tattone is along the outward route (**5h10min**), but don't forget to add on the extra times if you continue up the GR20 beyond the *bergerie* or you take the detour towards the Refuge de l'Onda.

7 VENACO • LUGO • ZUCCHERO • PONTE DI NOCETA • NOCETA • VIVARIO

See map on reverse of touring map; see also photograph page 80

Distance/time: 17.5km/11mi; 7h35min

Grade: moderate to strenuous, with a short but steep, gravelly descent at the start, and a long ascent of 580m/1900ft midway. Dangerous if wet. Don't attempt in changeable weather. Possibility of vertigo.

Equipment: walking boots, sunhat, sunglasses, suncream, long-sleeved shirt, long trousers, cardigan, anorak, raingear, picnic, water, swimwear

How to get there: 🚃 to Venaco (Timetable 21), or 🚌 (Timetable 7)
To return: same train from Vivario, or 🚌 (Timetable 7)

Short walks

1 Venaco — Ponte di Noceta — Venaco (moderate; 4h15min). Leave the main walk just before the Ponte di Noceta: follow signs for Venaco. Some 15min along the path, join an old track. 8min later, when the track swings sharply up to the right, continue straight ahead on a signposted path, alongside a stone wall. Ignore all branch-offs. 50min from the D43 cross a stream. Meet the D43 again and bear left. 75m/yds along, turn off right (on a driveway), then continue up the concrete lane, bearing right at the fork. Come to a street in Venaco and follow it uphill to a T-junction. Here bear right downhill for the train or left uphill for the bus (flag it down outside the pizzeria; Timetable 7).

2 Vivario — Muracciole — Vivario (easy; 2h). 🚌 (Timetable 7) or 🚃 to and from Vivario (Timetable 21). From the church walk up the N193 for 2min and then fork left on the D343 to Muracciole. Bear left. 100m/yds along turn left downhill on a rough track. Cross a bridge and, at the end of the track, bear right and continue on a path. Dog alert here! Descend through trees and soon cross a railway line, continuing on the path. After a second stream crossing, climb the hillside, keeping left. 8min uphill reach a vineyard and continue straight up. Go right at a junction, and go right again to round a building; then bear left immediately. Pass to the left of the Santa Maria chapel and keep straight on to Muracciole (55min). Return the same way.

Alternative walk: Venaco — Santo-Pietro-di-Venaco — Codopratu — Tatarellu — Santo-Pietro (very strenuous, with an ascent of over 1000m/3300ft; 6h10min). This route is marked with a dashed green line on the map. Although waymarking is at times obscure, I highly recommend this walk *for the adventurous*. 🚃 to Venaco (Timetable 21) and 🚌 from the N193 below Santo-Pietro to return (Timetable 7); flag it down! Or 🚗 to/from Santo-Pietro, thus saving 1h.

Traipsing along and over ridges, you cross unkempt hills foraged by a handful of cows and goats; otherwise you're all alone. An inviting pool awaits the swimmer; a profusion of spring flowers greets the botanist; superb scenery entices the photographer; the Vecchiu lures the fisherman. But for all that, I'm sorry to say that after the absolutely spectacular train ride to Venaco, the walk may be a bit of an anti-climax!

When you get off the train, Venaco lies behind you and Lugo in front of you. **Start out** by following the rail lines towards Lugo, and branch off left into the trees on a path 100m/yds along. In **8min** you're in Lugo. Follow the village lane downhill to the right. A circle of high ink-coloured hills is seen in the distance. Venaco sits across the valley in the shadows of a towering wall of grey rock. At the end of the village, and now on a path, come to a wooden cross and a sign for 'Ponte di Noceta'. Dashes of orange paint and small orange-coloured arrows waymark the route. Veer left and head down into the valley, passing plots and fruit trees. Cross a tiny bridge in a few minutes and, at a fork 50m/yds further on, go left. Ascending now, you enjoy a fine view of Venaco. Soon two short stretches of path may prove unnerving for less experienced walkers.

Rounding the ridge (**45min**), you come to the local incinerator (and surrounding earthworks). Your route swings up sharply left here: you cross the crest of the ridge and meet a road on the other side. Following signs for Ponte di Noceta, descend the road, heading right, and soon pass the transmitter station. Take the lower track that runs alongside this station. A little over five minutes down, turn off this track, descending a path to the left (**1h10min**). A minute later cut across the track again. The path then mounts the ridge, just above the track. A steady ascent follows, and you look down into the wide-open Tavignano Valley.

Soon you're back on the track again as it heads along the top of the crest. After a few minutes leave the track: turn off to the right and ascend a hump on the crest. Over the hump you descend to the forgotten outpost of Zucchero (**1h50min**), where you again meet the track you left earlier. From here head right for the Ponte di Noceta (signposted), descending into the maquis-matted valley. Less than 100m/yds down, fork off sharp left; a little further on, an arrow indicates that the way swings back again, to the right. This gravelly path drops rapidly. Take special care if it's at all damp.

At **2h20min** cross a stream, near a slate-roofed cottage. Eight minutes later, pass a derelict farmstead. Soon reach the D43, and turn left, alongside the noisy Vecchiu River. Some 100m/yds along, you pass the turn-off right to Venaco (Short walk 1).

The main walk continues by crossing the arched stone Ponte di Noceta. (Swimmers: a delightful — but deep — pool lies below the bridge.) Soon you'll see 'Noceta' written on the road. Turn off here and head through the gateway on the left. A few minutes up the

arm track, branch off right on a wide path cutting off
into the bushes. At the fork you encounter eight minutes
along, keep right for Noceta. (There are two paths turning off to the right here, one just before the small shady
stream, the other running alongside it. Take the latter.)
A little over ten minutes along watch for a path on your
right, heading up between stone walls. The entry point
is just before twin telephone poles. Here you leave the
stream and climb up to the Noceta road. Turn left on
the road (D43) and follow it for some 75m/yds, then
turn off left, onto a track signposted for Noceta. When
you reach a fork within five minutes, bear right uphill;
50m/yds along, bear right again, on a rough path.

Nearing **4h10min** you enter Noceta. Keep right.
Many mountain villages like Noceta are undergoing a
transformatiom: the old run-down houses are being
renovated and lived in once again. A couple of minutes
uphill through the houses you come to a fountain and a
charming old church. Head up the lane to the right of
the church. Some 200m/yds uphill you'll see a signpost
for Vivario and Muracciole. Leave the lane here: a gate
leads you onto a path climbing the hillside. Keep right
at the fork minutes up. You cross an unused track a
couple of times. Your panorama now extends across to
the Venaco side of the valley. In spring a great profusion of flowers entertains you with its colours — blue,
indigo, yellow, pink, and white.

At **5h15min** you cross the Col de Morello (also
called the Bocca Murellu; 824m/2700ft; see photograph page 80). Dropping down over this pass you're
soon alongside a stone wall, following an old mule track.

delightful deep pool awaits you here at the Ponte di Noceta.

(Watch for some detours that avoid overgrown stretches of track.) Vivario, your destination, comes into sight, ahead to your left, stretching across a wooded hillside. Monte d'Oro (Walk 5) rises sharply in the background.

Go through two junctions, keeping straight ahead (the left-hand fork). From fire-scarred slopes you come to the most picturesque part of the walk (**P7**). Muracciole lies ahead, crowned by its miniature château. Beyond an enchanting, crumbled hamlet (**6h05min**), a path signposted for Vivario joins from the right. But continue straight on: cross a small bridge draped in creepers and climb into Muracciole (**6h30min**). The place has a timeless air; it exudes charm. The château sits up behind the fountain.

Making for Vivario, return to the junction and bear left. In three minutes pass to the right of the solitary Santa Maria chapel. At another junction, under five minutes later, round a crumbled building to the right and, immediately beyond it, bear left. Go left again at the next junction, to descend a ridge. Tired stone walls flank the route. Soon you come to an enclosed vineyard. Midway along it, strike off abruptly left, sliding down into the narrow valley. Cross a stream and pick up your ongoing path on the other side. Cross another stream a minute later and then begin the ascent to Vivario, through a wood carpeted in cyclamen. Fifty minutes from Muracciole you emerge from the scrub and cross the railway. A wide path takes you up through a thin wood. Soon you join a bumpy track, just by a house where there are three large dogs who don't think you have the right of way! A steep 10-minute climb sees you in Vivario (**7h35min**). The bus stop lies two minutes to the right, on the N193, in front of the lovely village fountain. (If it's Sunday or a holiday, you'll have to catch the train. The station is 25 minutes downhill: take the first left turn.)

8 MARIGNANA • REVINDA • CARGESE

Distance/time: 30km/18.5mi; 11h30min

Grade: strenuous, especially on the final ascent (300m/985ft). There is also an ascent of 390m/1280ft at the start. Only recommended for the very fit. It's a long walk for one day, but if you take a sleeping sack and food, you could spend the night at the refuge in Revinda (gas for cooking is provided). Don't attempt in changeable weather; it can be extremely cold and slippery along this route.

Equipment: walking boots, sunhat, sunglasses, suncream, long trousers, long-sleeved shirt, cardigans, anorak, gloves, picnic, water

How to get there: 🚌 to Marignana (Timetable 3)
To return: 🚌 from Cargèse (Timetable 2)

Short walk: Cargèse — Lozzi (quite easy, but with a 1h05min ascent at the start; 2h30min). 🚌 to go and return (Timetable 2). Refer to the map on page 78 and follow the orange waymarking. Begin at the intersection just above Cargèse (on the D81). Take the road striking off right (the one heading up behind the large old fountain. Flag down the bus just opposite the point where you join the D81.

The exhilarating bus ride to Marignana puts you in the mood for this mammoth hike. The bus does most of the climbing; you do the descending. The bus driver, with his jocular manner, is as entertaining as the scenery. You'll trail across a desolate landscape of high rounded hills, where wild pigs roam, rooting for grubs. Extensive open views follow you all the way. But remember, you've got to be really fit for this outing!

Scramble out of the bus at the church in Marignana. Across from the church, you'll see an alley cutting back into the houses. An orange arrow marks the entrance, and **the walk starts here.** Head up the alley, following the orange dots and dashes. A good minute up, reach the road.

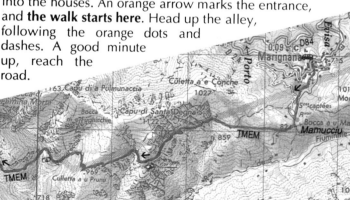

Some 70m/yds uphill to the left, take the first turn-off to the right. This small scattered village is an interesting mixture of old and renovated houses. The surrounding slopes are wooded in chestnuts. Passing under the archway of a lovely old home, you leave Marignana for the trees (keep right). Stay on the left-hand side of the stream. You'll come onto a faint track and join another track meeting you from the right. Bear left and, 100m/yds further on, fork off to the right. Then, almost immediately, swing right onto another track. Some **40min** along, you turn off again, going left onto a well-marked path (a rock just inside it is marked 'Revinda'). Shortly, you cross over a ridge, and the coast comes into view far below. Scrub-covered, rocky hills rise all around you; strawberry trees, heather, *Cistus*, and thorny broom lie scattered across the slopes. At the **1h15min**-mark stretches of cobble-stones suggest the remains of an old path.

At **1h40min**, descending the very steep Culletta a u Prunu, you pass your first landmark — a small stone building set in a grove of broken old chestnut trees. There's a water source just behind it. Cross over small mountain streams cascading down the hillsides. A noticeable ascent follows, as you mount a crest. A magnificent panorama awaits you: rows of hills rolling down off the central mountain chain to the sea. Wild pigs have rooted up the soft ground along the way. Tiny alpine violets appear on the side of the path.

At about **3h20min** a grassy pass (the Bocca d'Acquaviva; 1102m/3615ft) takes you over into the Riogna Valley, a deep V. Notice the twin granite peaks across from you and, behind you, a fine view of Corsica's snow-glazed summits. Fifteen minutes below the pass, you come to an old pastoral outpost (*bergerie*) and some cows that look nearly as ancient. This grassy patch is a good place to stop for lunch.

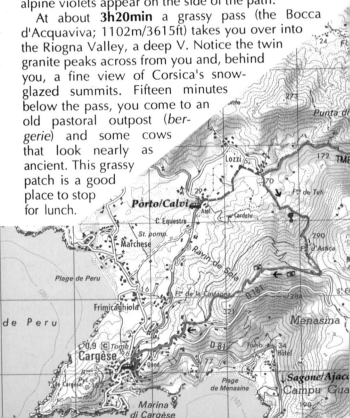

Just below the derelict buildings, the path swings right. Slip and slide your way down into the valley. Around one hour downhill, you come to the river. And from here on, you will meander around the hillsides, through the forest. This is the most beautiful stretch of the walk. Crossing a side-stream, you leave the Forêt de Marignana and enter the Forêt Caus de Curstinace.

Ascending a shady path (referring now to the map below), meet an enclosure (**6h**). Pass through a gate and follow the fence on your right. When the path forks, go left. The

hamlet of Revinda is off to the right and comes into sight through the trees. Sitting on the tail of a ridge, high above a plain, it looks out over the beautiful horseshoe Bay of Chiuni. Revinda's refuge (photograph page 80) is met at close on **6h40min**, set on a scrub-cluttered hillside, and with a fine outlook over the Bay of Chiuni. Eight minutes from the refuge, a rocky perch provides unimpeded views. The waymarked trail leads you into a very steep, slippery descent into the Esigna Valley, where you come upon a *bergerie* (**8h**) near the valley floor. Join a track and bear left along it, soon crossing the valley floor. At the junction that follows turn right and remain on this track for the next hour.

The refuge at Revinda, where you could spend the night.

At about **9h15min**, below Lozzi, you turn off left for Cargèse (signposted). Thirty-five minutes uphill, a very short stretch of path is vertiginous. Pass a turn-off to the left. Skirting a farm, you cross its track (between two gates) and continue up the hill, to a large house. Leave through a gate (**10h15min**), bear right immediately, and then circle the house, following the garden wall. Notice the scant remains of an ancient church on your left. Off the ridge there are superb views over the Capo di Feno (Walk 1), and north to the sharply outlined Capu Rossu. Passing through fields, you soon descend the right-hand flank of the ridge. At **10h55min** cross a track and go right, on another track. Minutes later, fork right onto a path. When you reach a track signposted 'Depart Tra Mare e Monti', bear left to join a small road. Head down it to the right, then go right again at the next junction. At the main road, go left to Cargèse centre (**11h30min**). The bus leaves from the post office.

A great many walking routes are signposted. This is the Bocca Murellu (Col de Morello; Walk 7).

9 EVISA TO OTA (SPELUNCA GORGE)

Distance/time: 6km/3.8mi; 2h05min   **See also photograph page 84**

Grade: easy, but with a steep (although not difficult) descent of 650m/ 2100ft. Dangerous if wet. Slight possibility of vertigo.

Equipment: sturdy shoes or walking boots, sunhat, sunglasses, sun-cream, long-sleeved shirt, long trousers, cardigan, anorak, rainwear, swimwear, picnic, water

How to get there: 🚌 to Evisa (Timetable 3)
To return: 🚌 from Ota (Timetable 2)

A short and relatively easy walk, this excursion takes you to the Gorges de Spelunca — a must for every visitor to Corsica. Imposing buttresses of pink-hued rock bursting up out of the valley dominate the landscape. Deep in the gorge, you wander alongside a tumbling river, crossed by old arched footbridges. In summer you'll be tempted to take a swim in one of the inviting pools. The walk ends in the delightful village of Ota, set in majestic countryside (see page 84).

You'll spend more time on buses getting to and from the walk, than actually walking... but the journey is through such superb landscapes that you can look forward to a 'perfect day'. Get off the bus in Evisa, a village set high in the mountains, in a cloak of chestnut trees. **Start out** by following the road back downhill towards Porto for about ten minutes, until you reach the cemetery. Already you will have noticed the rose-tinted granite peaks rising up out of the landscape.

Immediately past the enclosed part of the cemetery your path (signposted 'Ota-Evisa'), cuts back off the road to the right and descends into the gorge far below. You dip down into a maquis wood sprinkled with pines, through which you can see the hillside village of Ota with its red-tiled roofs. Pink crags overshadow it. In the distance, the valley winds down to the sea. This path (slippery when wet) descends very steeply. Moss coats the surrounding trees, and the banks are flecked with cyclamen. Looking back, to the right, you see a bald mound of shiny grey rock bulging out of the summits. Soon precipitous, scrub-covered walls tower above you. About **1h** downhill, cross a side-stream on the beautifully-cobbled Pont (Bridge) de Zaglia (*P9*), shown on the next page. Alders lean over it. The stream joins a fast-flowing river just below the bridge, and you may be tempted to swim. Soon the Capu di Larata (1193m/3915ft), Ota's guardian, holds your attention.

At the **1h25min**-mark, you come onto the D124, just above a couple of pretty stone bridges, 'les Deux Ponts

The Genoese Pont de Zaglia, one of the settings for Picnic 9.

d'Ota'. Some 80m/yds *before* crossing the bridges, head down left into the valley floor again, on a concrete lane. Circle a football pitch to the right to return to the path, soon rejoining the river. A little over ten minutes below the road, you cross the river on a perfectly-restored, splendid Genoese footbridge, the Ponte Vecchiu (*P9*). The pool it crosses is ideal for swimming. Over the bridge, swing left, head through a gate, and follow the river. Two mountains of rock thrusting up from the valley

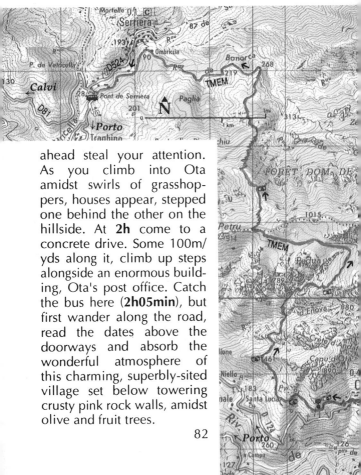

ahead steal your attention. As you climb into Ota amidst swirls of grasshoppers, houses appear, stepped one behind the other on the hillside. At **2h** come to a concrete drive. Some 100m/yds along it, climb up steps alongside an enormous building, Ota's post office. Catch the bus here (**2h05min**), but first wander along the road, read the dates above the doorways and absorb the wonderful atmosphere of this charming, superbly-sited village set below towering crusty pink rock walls, amidst olive and fruit trees.

82

10 OTA TO SERRIERA

Distance/time: 12.5km/7.75mi; 5h

Grade: strenuous, with a 595m/1950ft ascent at the start (2h30min), much of it very steep. The descent (885m/2900ft) is also very steep, and dangerous if wet. Only for the very fit. Possibility of vertigo.

Equipment: walking boots, sunhat, sunglasses, suncream, long trousers, cardigan, anorak, raingear, swimwear, picnic, water

How to get there: 🚌 to Ota (Timetable 2)

To return: same bus from *Porto*. In high season (15/5-15/10) you can catch a bus to Porto on the D81 at the Serriera turn-off (Timetable 8); otherwise you will have to walk (add 1h40min), or arrange for a taxi. **NB:** If you're based at Ajaccio, this walk demands an overnight stay in Porto. In peak season, reserve accommodation well in advance.

You set out overlooking the luxuriant, tree-smothered Porto Valley, and you end up in a landscape of dark rolling hills. In between, the route clambers up through a gap in the hills, where lofty, rose-coloured rock walls look down on you. All along the way you catch glimpses of the stunning Porto Gulf, of pink granite sea-bluffs, secluded coves and deep blue sea.

The bus stops outside the post office in Ota, the charming hillside village shown on the next page. **Start out** by walking back the way the bus came: in minutes you'll see, on your right, a wide stone-paved path. It's a section of the 'Mare e Monti' route, so is waymarked with orange paint. Follow it; it becomes a concrete lane. After bearing left into a driveway, you swing up behind the last houses, pass through a gate, and you're on path once again. (A short strip of path 15 minutes beyond the gate may prove difficult for inexperienced walkers.)

Superb views encompass you. Already high up, you look straight across the valley. Chestnut groves sprinkled across the slopes cheer up the dark countryside. Before you head around the hillside, take a moment to look back at Ota, with its bright orange-tiled rooftops and bib of grey-green olive trees. Soon Porto comes into view, trickling down to the sea alongside the final stretch of the Porto River. At the end of the village you can see a rock crowned with an ancient tower jutting into the sea. Minutes later, bear right at the junction.

At just over **50min**, you mount a ridge and look over into a narrow side-valley, where walls of rose-coloured

rock seem to block your way. Looking back you soon catch a glimpse of Porto's picture-postcard beach. Troupes of pink-flowering foxgloves flourish on rubble-strewn patches of hillside. Zigzagging back into this 'pink' valley, you scramble up through a narrow gap in rock walls, where the scent of the pale mauve-to-blue rosemary plants may surround you. At around **2h20min** the path swings sharply uphill to the left, near the edge of the ridge. Just to the right you have a fine outlook over Porto's valley: the dome-shaped Capu d'Orto (Walk 11) dominates the landscape. Continuing up through pines and heather, you come into a spacious chestnut grove. A fountain is passed en route, and a small stone building, up on the rocky hillock of Pedua to the left.

At about **3h** you pass a sign 'Bocca San Petru, 900m'. A nearly vertical descent follows ... possibly on your backside. The countryside ahead eases out into smooth rolling hills but, inland, peaks still capped with snow appear in the distance. Further downhill, you spot the striking Bussaglia Beach, sprawling across the mouth of the wide, gravelly bed of the Vetricella.

At a little over **3h20min**, clambering down a rocky ridge, you look straight down into Serriera. The village is as red as the hillside rock from which it was built. Pass through a lovely glade and then come out onto a track; remain on it all the way to the main road, fifty minutes down (**5h**). (The 'Mare e Monte' footpath turns off some thirty-five minutes along, but you do *not*.) Porto is left. A bus stop is 200m/yds up to your right, at the Serriera turn-off (see 'To return' on page 83).

The charming village of Ota, dominated by the Capu di Larata. Walk 9 ends here, and Walk 10 begins here. The pink granite rock walls here in the upper reaches of the Porto Valley create one of Corsica's most beautiful landscapes.

11 PONT DE MEZANU • CAPU D'ORTO • BOCCA LARGA • LES CALANCHE

See also photograph page 32

Distance/time: 11km/6.75mi; 6h05min

Grade: Strenuous climb of 825m/2700ft, the final part of which (to the Capu d'Orto; 1294m/4245ft) is only recommended for *experts*. Very dangerous in wet conditions; do not attempt in bad weather. Can be cold. Possibility of vertigo. Less experienced walkers should omit the summit and follow the notes from the 3h45min-point.

Equipment: walking boots, sunhat, sunglasses, suncream, gloves, long-sleeved shirt, long trousers, warm jacket, cardigan, anorak, raingear, picnic, water

How to get there: 🚌 to the Pont de Mezanu at Piana (Timetable 2) *To return:* same bus, from les Roches Bleues

Short walk: to le Château Fort and return (40min; easy but awkward, with lots of ups and downs, clambering over rock.) 🚌 to the 'Chemin du Château' (Timetable 2). The path is waymarked and well trodden. Leave from the lay-by/parking area. Nothing remains of the old château, but the walk is well worth while for the sea views and the superb vista over les Calanche. See photograph page 87.

Alternative walk: Pont de Mezanu — Foce d'Orto — Pont de Mezanu (moderate; 4h10min). Follow the main walk as far as the junction met at 1h15min (where the word 'fontaine' is carved on a rock on the side of the path). Here keep right for the Foce d'Orto and, at the faint fork met 15min later, bear left. Eight minutes uphill you're at the Foce d'Orto — a gap in the giant mounds of rock. From here you have wonderful views of the inland hills and the village of Evisa, set high on a plateau. On your return, follow the main walk for the rest of the way, ignoring the turn-off for the Capu d'Orto.

This walk turns les Calanche inside-out for you. This natural phenomenon of weird and wonderful, weather-sculpted rock, shown in the photograph on page 32, is found nowhere else on Corsica. Heading inland from the Calanche, the landscape changes again, and you wind your way around massive, bulky mounds of bare pink and grey rock. From the summit of the Capu d'Orto you will enjoy the unsurpassed views over the Gulf of Porto and into the rugged interior shown on page 86. (On discovering that Michelin only gave this view two stars, I threw the book away.) It's a 5-star view in my book — don't you agree?

The track where **the walk begins** is the first turn-off to the right, just north of the bridge (Pont de Mezanu). Some 50m/yds uphill, you'll see green and orange waymarks on a pole on your left. For the moment, follow the orange waymarks: turn right at the fork ahead. You enter a V-shaped valley lined with rocky hills. The inclines on your left are pink; those to the right are grey. The Capu di u Vitullu (1330m/4360ft) is the impressive mountain of rock dominating the right-hand side of the valley. The Capu d'Orto is still hidden from sight by the ever-billowing mounds of rock on your left. *Asphodelu* and sprinklings of lavender and *Cistus* grow on the open slopes, while heather crowds underneath the pines. Keep left at the fork **15min** along. At around **35min** uphill, the track ends. Two paths continue off it yours is the wide cobbled one to the right (waymarked) Heather and strawberry trees flank the way, and the path narrows as you ascend into pines. Within the next 15 minutes, pass a faint turn-off to the left. Some 25 minutes (**1h15min**) later, come to a junction, where the word 'fontaine' is carved into a rock by the side of the path. The Alternative walk continues up to the right here, but the main walk branches off left for the Capu d'Orto. Soon bushes of wild rosemary, with their pale marine-blue blooms and strongly-scented leaves, capture your attention. You head across a wooded basin, the path becoming more like a watercourse.

Close on **1h40min**, meet the Capu d'Orto turn-off, to the right. A large rock splashed with green paint way-marking, alerts you to it. Now you have to scramble up the rose-coloured rock, brushing through clumps of rosemary and watching out for the green waymarking and the small piles of stones that mark the route. *Steady*

From the Capu d'Orto: for me, this is the most breath-taking viewpoint on the island. Porto sits far below, the whole gulf lit up by its beach. A rugged coastline twirls its way north, leaving behind small coves.

Looking west along the coast and over the Anse de Ficajola, from the ruins of the Château Fort (Short walk). Les Calanche are hidden from view by the giant pillar of rock in the foreground.

footwork is required from here on. Bizzare rock formations grow up around you, their colours intensifying. After eight minutes' scrambling, the impressive peak confronts you, bulging straight up out of the landscape. A fine veil of bright green lichen covers the rock face, which is separated from you by a shallow neck of pine-collared rock. Two paths drop down towards the pines; you can use either. Now the real climb begins.

At just under **2h15min** you're below a slight groove cutting up the hillside. 'Capu d'Orto' appears in faded paint on the rock, and an arrow points straight up. From here on the way is marked only by small piles of rocks. If you don't enjoy scrambling up a steep rock face (especially with the prospect of the vertiginous descent on your return), call it quits here and just lap up the view. The heights of the Calanche bump their way seaward, getting more unruly and expressive as they go. Beyond this realm of pink rock, you see Piana wrapped in greenery, nestling high on a crest.

Those climbing to the summit will find that tackling this 'groove' is an all-fours job. Just when you think you're almost there, the twin-breasted top of the peak looms up ahead ... still 25 minutes away! You cross a small grassy shelf tucked back into the peak, and then the final assault follows, often with the help of your hands. *Make sure all the rocks you stand on or lean against are secure!* In the cleavage of the split peak, you clamber *carefully* up onto the right-hand protrusion. And at around **2h45min** you're on the summit. The view is the most breath-taking that I have seen on all my walks on Corsica. Not only do you overlook Porto's sweep of beach and tower (see photograph opposite) but, inland, great rounded hills roll back one onto the other. Evisa is seen, set on a plateau back in the hills. To the southwest, the vista stretches as far as the bays of Cargèse — the Gulfs of Chiuni and Péru. A little further along to the right, you peer down onto Ota, resting at the foot of an amphitheatre of rose-coloured rock.

Descend back to the turn-off point (**3h45min**), and head right, following the green dots. At a junction met some minutes later, keep straight on (the right-hand fork). You get another glimpse of Piana, this time framed between rocky outcrops and flowering scrub. Passing through a neat stone wall (**4h45min**), the bay reappears through trees. Just below lies a dell of chestnuts and pines, where you encounter, and ignore, a turn-off to the right. A few minutes beyond the dell, a confusing intersection comes up. Continue straight on through it (that is, take the left-hand fork). Soon you're looking down into the valley you ascended at the start of the walk.

Approaching **5h20min**, and descending through an open clearing thick with *Cistus* and heather, your way forks. If you've left a car at the start of the walk, follow the *green* arrows here, heading left (make sure not to miss more arrows a couple of minutes down, where the path suddenly cuts back to the left). Otherwise leave the path here and fork off to the right, following the *blue* dots and arrows.

The rest of the walk is nothing less than spectacular. the blue dots lead you down to the right. When a path crosses in front of you (a minute down), turn right along it; it's an old mule trail. Ignore the turn-off to the left that follows. Soon after rounding the ridge, you're greeted by the 'mouth-watering' view shown on page 32 — the Calanche (**P**11). If it's evening, plonk yourself down and take in a sunset you'll long remember. A very steep convoluted descent drops you onto the road at just over the **6h**-mark. (This descent is dangerous if wet.) Five minutes downhill to the right along the road, you'll find a bar/souvenir shop at les Roches Bleues (**6h05min**). Flag down your bus here.

Distance/time: 11km/6.8mi; 5h10min

Grade: Strenuous, with an ascent of 700m/2300ft. Very dangerous in wet weather. Inexperienced walkers: use the map to ascend and descend via Petra Maio; see footnote page 91. Possibility of vertigo.

Equipment: walking boots, sunhat, sunglasses, suncream, long trousers, long-sleeved shirt, cardigan, anorak, raingear, picnic, water

How to get there and return: The walk begins and ends in Calvi.

Short walk: Calvi — Notre Dame de la Serra — Calvi (fairly strenuous, but very short; 1h55min). Follow the main walk to the chapel (12) and return the same way.

Alternative walk: Calvi — la Revellata — Calvi (easy; 3h45min). Leave Calvi on the Porto road. Turn down the first fork to the right (signposted 'l'Oasis'; 15min). A minute down, take the dirt track off to the left, heading below wooden holiday bungalows. At the entrance to the Residences l'Oasis, turn off left, onto a driveway. The path continues straight off it. 20min later come to a cove. Pick up a track on the other side of the cove, and follow it along the coast. When it peters out, keep to the path along the shore. Ignore all routes climbing inland. Having passed a few lovely pebbly coves, you reach the largest of them (1h). Here climb up towards the lighthouse. Minutes up,

leave the path (just before it dips down and becomes impassable), and zigzag up a faint path, to a gravel road (7min up). Bear right on the road and right again at a fork (100m/yds further on). Pass through the entrance to the lighthouse and the Marine Biology Research Centre (private property, but access on foot is allowed; to visit, telephone Mr Bay: 95.65.06.18). The building is straight on.

Return the same way or via the lighthouse road (see dashed lines on the map).

From start to finish, you have sweeping views over t Calvi Gulf. Scaling great swellings of hillside roc and pushing your way through perfumed maquis, yo reach the summit of the Capu di a Veta (703m/2305 From here you have a magnificent view over the g and the amphitheatre of hills behind it.

The walk starts in Calvi, at the youth hostel on t Avenue de la République (5 on the town plan, page ! Just south of the hostel, turn up a street signposted 'R de Porto (bord de mer)'. Follow signs for 'Hotel Res dence les Aloes'. Take the first left, then the first rig and circle the stadium (ignore the street off to the righ When the road forks (just past a roundabout), keep le Pass a turn to the right, then watch out for a small si 'Notre Dame de la Serra', in an alley on your left. directs you along a passageway. Soon climb steps ov smooth rock. Continue straight ahead: you can now s the chapel, Notre-Dame de la Serra. Pass through field, then turn down left to a road. Turn right on th road, and climb past the Hotel La Villa (ignore the le turn before it). You are now on the 'Chemin de N-D c la Serra'. Not far above the hotel pass through a jun tion and continue straight up. Five minutes beyond th junction, look for a track cutting off to the left. It's easi missed, but a house sits opposite the turn-off. The stee track snakes up to the chapel, shown opposite (**1h**; *P*12

Leave the chapel the way you entered it, and hea left along the main track, towards the Capu di a Vet. At the fork 100m/yds along, bear right. At the next fork eight minutes later, go left. The peak, adorned with cross, fills the picture ahead. Another fork follows with in fifteen minutes; bear right. At **1h40min** the motorabl track ends, and a rough lane continues on, swingin back to the left. Follow it; it's a steep climb. The lan fizzles out at a pass overlooking a severe, rocky valley Continue on the faint path opposite the nearby powe pylon. Head straight up, ignoring a path off left.

You climb through a narrow passage in the ridge small piles of stones keeping you in line. These stone as well as dashes of wine-red or yellow paint, mark th way from here on. Once through the gap, you descend briefly. Scrambling round the rocky hillside, you edg along a ledge, where the going is a bit vertiginous. requires a keen eye to follow the waymarkers. G carefully and *watch out for loose stones*. Just over 1. minutes off the track, you come out to a cleavage in th

The chapel of Notre Dame de la Serra (Picnic 12), with the Capu di a Veta in the background. From its rocky plinth the chapel commands a superb outlook over Calvi and the gulf, and inland up the river delta to the central spine of mountains. Founded in the 15th century, the chapel is only open on the th of September, to celebrate the Feast of the Nativity of the Virgin Mary.

dge and have views on both des: Calvi and the Gulf to the ft and the unspoilt turquoise ichiareto Bay to your right. ght minutes later your views xpand to encompass the enlosing arm of the Calvi Gulf — the Punta Spano. umio (Walk 13) is on the hills across the bay.

Ascending, remain on the left side of Veta's inclines. 2h45min you reach the summit, the Capu di a Veta, vhere you can sit back and take in this aerial view over ne gulfs and surrounding hills. Mount Cinto, the land's highest point, is the shark's fin-shaped peak nat rises out of the backbone of mountains. The igarella and Fiume Seccu river plains spread out into a ast fan around the bay.

Descending, take an easier route. Heading in the lirection of Mount Cinto, see a two-way arrow pointing ut your continuation, a route clearly marked with red nd white paint. Facing Calvi, descend the right-hand lank of the peak. Fork left some eight minutes down. Come to the junction for the Capu di a Conca, fifteen minutes down. Calvi is left. You drop quickly, through a nass of vegetation (keep straight on all the way down). Pass two turn-offs to the left.*

At **4h** the path appears to come out onto the end of a road; but in fact turns sharply right, descending into the bed of the valley, where you cross the stream and bear left. A minute above the stream pass a turn-off right for another peak. Eight minutes after going through a gap in a stone wall, you come onto a track. Follow it to a road on the outskirts of Petra Maio. Keep right at the junction here, left at the next two, then pass a turn off left, and keep straight on all the way to the main road. Calvi lies along to the left (**5h10min**).

*If you are doing the walk in reverse, you pass these two turn-offs (on your right): the first has the word 'normal' written in large red letters, the second is waymarked with yellow paint. Keep left at both forks.

13 LUMIO • OCCI • LAVATOGGIO • SANT' ANTONINO • L'ILE-ROUSSE

Distance/time: 18km/11.25mi; 6h25min

Grade: moderate, with a 35-minute steep ascent (280m/920ft) at t'
start. Within the reach of any sturdy hill walker. Slippery when wet.

Equipment: walking boots, sunhat, sunglasses, suncream, swimwea
long trousers, long-sleeved shirt, cardigan, anorak, raingear, picni
water

How to get there: 🚐 taxi to the Hotel/Restaurant 'Chez Charles' (c
the north side of Lumio, at the right-hand side of the N197 whe
coming from Calvi; 10km). Or 🚌 to Ondari (Timetable 12), fro
where you can walk to Lumio (head straight up the road from th
station and turn left on the N197 to 'Chez Charles'; 1h05min).
To return: 🚌 from l'Ile-Rousse (Timetable 12)

Discover the enchanting villages of the Balagne o
foot. Each has a personality of its own and is ric
in history. For a change you don't have to climb hur
dreds of metres for an unforgettable view; wonderfu
rural vistas accompany you all along these little hill
This country trail is spiced with an intriguing deserte
village, a quiet tucked-away grassy valley where foxe
roam, and — best of all — a mouth-watering restauran
If you ignore the sad wounds of the summer fires tha
plague this island, you'll have a perfect rambling day.

Just south of Chez Charles, a road turns off int
Lumio. A large parking bay is inside the road. A lan
called the 'Chemin de Zappol' forks off the road, jus
before a shop. **Start out** by heading left up this lane
When it ends outside a house (**3min**), continue briefly
on a faint track and then a goats' path flanked by tire
stone walls. A couple of minutes up, turn off right or
another path (waymarked with a small orange dot on a
wall). A very steep climb awaits you. When you pause
to catch your breath, you can enjoy a tremendous view
over the white sandy beach and the bay, to Calvi and la
Revellata (the lighthouse promontory; Alternative walk
12). In **15min**, just after you have clambered over a
shaky fence, the way evens out briefly, and you look
down over the turquoise waters of Marine de Sant'
Ambrogio. Minutes further on, pass through a crumbled

tone wall and enter the precincts of Occi. As you head across an enclosed grassy field, you'll see the high walls of its derelict buildings begin to appear over the hill. Keep to the right of them, and you're soon in this mysterious, abandoned village, where you can sit on the slopes and contemplate the bay below.

Beyond Occi you may notice faint spots of red paint on rocks beside the path, as well as small piles of stones marking the way. Ascending towards the peak, keep slightly to the right of it. At **40min**, not far below the Capu d'Occi, you clamber through a fence and, a minute later, head back through it again. Beyond a wheat-threshing floor and over the crest lies an elevated open valley that empties out onto the plains below Lumio. Walls smothered in *Cistus* run down and across the hills, tel-ling of intensive cultivation in the past. A couple of herds-men's igloo-like stone huts rest on the slopes below. The inconspicuous cha-pel of Notre Dame de la Stella, revealed by its red-tiled roof, sits on the valley floor. Descending on various animal trails through dense scrub, now make

for this cha-pel. There are paths to the left and to the right but, as long as you can *see* the chapel, you'll reach it easily. (If it's misty, walk over to the wall on your left and head straight downhill beside it; it will keep you on

course.) In **1h05min** you're alongside the chapel
Peeking inside you'll see that it is clean and cared for.

Heading on to Lavatoggio, follow the track to the
left. At around **1h40min** pass alongside another chapel.
The way becomes a concrete lane, and you soon
descend into a splendid valley sprinkled with old
tightly-knit villages. The most noticeable of these is
Sant' Antonino, strategically perched high on a knoll.
Algajola Beach, a gently curving bay (at present free of
buildings) comes into view next. The valley floor is a
chessboard of hayfields. Fifteen minutes from the last
chapel, come out onto the D71, just below Lavatoggio,
a sleepy, shuttered village with some large mansions.
Follow the cobbled lane around the church and up to
the square, to get a taste of the place, and then head
down to the main road. Turn right and make for Cateri.

The Couvent de Marcasso comes into sight below
the road. This well-maintained 17th-century building
sits alone on a terraced hillside, overlooking Algajola
Bay. Leave the road after fifteen minutes: at the signposted turn-off for the convent, bear right for Cateri
(**2h30min**). This charming village overlooks a garden of
fruit trees. Tall old granite houses huddle around the
church. Ancient stone walls line the cobbled lane,
which you soon join. Half a minute down it, you'll see
the 'Poste & Telecommunications' building. The alley
forking off right alongside this building will lead you
out of the village … but first you may decide to treat
yourself at the local *auberge*. Once you get a whiff of
what's on the day's menu, it's almost impossible to con-
vince yourself that all you want is your picnic!

Following the alley by the post office, you
circle the back of the church (which houses
interesting paintings on its ceiling and an elabo-
rate marble altar) to join the D151 in about eight
minutes. Turn left for Sant' Antonino. A little over
five minutes along, fork right on the D413. Less
than 25 minutes up the road, opposite a farm
building, turn off right on a wide stone-paved
path to the village. Keep right all the way up.

Standing like a citadel fortifying the hilltop,
Sant' Antonino (*P*13) is at its most impressive
from this approach. Enter it at **3h20min**, through
low dark archways. From the top of the rock, you
look down into courtyards and alleys and have a
fine panorama over the settled countryside.

Monte Grosso (1938m/6355ft) stands out behind you, rising up out of a wall of high hills.

Once you've had your fill of views and found your way to the large church on the plateau at the foot of the village, make for l'Ile Rousse. Some 50m/yds along the road, fork right on a dirt track that cuts across the small grassy plateau below Sant' Antonino. Stone walls flank the route, which passes the turn-off to the cemetery. The Moorish village of Corbara catches your eye, set on a slope on the tail of this ridge. After 15 minutes, the track forks. (The Capu Corbinu, a 15-minute optional detour to the right, provides a good viewpoint over l'Ile-Rousse and the surrounding countryside.) The main walk continues to the left. You're soon looking down on the beautiful 'Red Island'. An inviting stretch of beach, the Plage de Botre, captures your attention next.

Meet the D263 and bear right for Occiglioni, coming into the village in eight minutes (**4h45min**). Here take the cobbled path descending to the left from the parking bay. Keep straight all the way downhill, ignoring any forks. Eight minutes down you pass a lovely old fountain. Twenty minutes down join a track, pass a house, and then bear right off the track, to rejoin the path. At a confusion of paths below a charming stone cottage, continue straight ahead. On reaching the N197 (**6h**), turn right to l'Ile Rousse. (If you are doing the walk in reverse, this turn-off is immediately beyond a disco/pub on your left.) The town centre is down to the right; the station is west of the beach (**6h25min**).

Sant' Antonino — masterpiece of the Balagne

14 CALENZANA TO BONIFATU

Distance/time: 11km/6.8mi; 4h   **Map continues on pages 98-9**
Grade: moderate, with a short ascent of 326m/1070ft
Equipment: walking boots, sunhat, sunglasses, suncream, swimwear, long trousers, long-sleeved shirt, cardigan, anorak, raingear, water, picnic
How to get there: 🚖 taxi from Calvi to Calenzana (12.5km), or 🚌 to Calenzana (Timetable 10), in *high season only*
To return: 🚖 same taxi from Bonifatu to Calvi (arrange in advance)

This hike follows the start of the island's 'Tra Mare e Monti' ('Sea and Mountains') footpath and is easily accesssible to all energetic hill walkers. Sadly, forest fires have scarred much of the countryside. In spring, however, the maquis is a tangled bouquet of colour. The Figarella River, alongside which you climb as you near Bonifatu, will probably entice you to spend the rest of the day there with its inviting and invigorating pools. But ... as this hike is relatively easy, and short, you may like to combine it with Walk 15.

You **begin this walk** winding through picturesque Calenzana, an important centre in the Genoese epoch. Leave the village from the 17th/18th-century church of St-Blaise (note the elegant campanile): head up past the church, keeping an eye out for the GR20 waymarks, which are not very obvious. Pass a parking area on your right and disappear amongst the houses. Within **5min**, when the street ends, continue on a lane for 25m/yds. Then fork left, soon passing a renovated fountain. Signs for the GR20 and the 'Tra Mare e Monti' follow. (For the first hour or so both walks follow the same route, an old trail that climbs straight up into the hills.)

The GR20 forks off left at just under the **1h**-mark;

Mists swirl around the peaks at Bonifatu and Calenzana.

keep right. You look out over the flat-bottomed valley of the Fiume Seccu. Once over the crest (Bocca u Corsu; 581m/1900ft) you drop down into the vast, tapering Figarella Valley, just where it disappears into the central massif. In **1h50min,** not long after the third stream crossing, you come to a track and head up to the left for Bonifatu (signposted). Remain on this track, keeping straight all the way. Beyond a turn-off to the left, you look up into rocky mountains.

Now the valley closes up, and the river is not far below; cross it at **3h 05min** (see map on pages 98-99). Here you leave the track and follow the river, turning left up a wide signposted path. Scramble along the old watercourse, briefly floundering across rocks and boulders. At just under **3h30min** you pass close to some inviting pools. They draw you to a halt, and you soon forget the time. The further upstream you go, the more delightful the pools. Cool off, then bake yourself dry on one of the gigantic boulders! There's no need to hurry; the walk ends only 35 minutes further uphill.

A rough 15-minute ascent brings you onto the Bonifatu road; the *auberge* lies another 15 minutes up, to your left. You now look up into a striking valley framed by mountains. High above the treeline, bare and forbidding crags rise abruptly. Far below, green pools sit cradled in the valley floor. Soon you come to a forestry house, the Maison Forêt de Bonifatu and, two minutes later, the Auberge de la Forêt. The road ends here, as does the walk (**4h; P**15). But if this dramatic scenery leaves you still thirsting for more, turn to Walk 15.

15 BONIFATU • REFUGE DE CARROZZU • SPASIMATA SWINGBRIDGE • BONIFATU

Distance/time: 12km/7.5mi; 4h30min

Grade: fairly strenuous, with an ascent of 620m/2035ft lasting two hours. Not suitable in cold or changeable weather. While the descent to the bridge might prove unnerving for some, *I heartily recommend this walk for everyone who is fit and sure-footed — even beginners.*

Equipment: walking boots, sunhat, sunglasses, suncream, swimwear, long trousers, long-sleeved shirt, gloves, cardigan, warm jacket, raingear, picnic, water, waders

How to get there and return: 🚍 taxi from Calvi to the auberge at Bonifatu (22km); arrange to be collected there at the end of the day.

You scale the wall of a deep valley in the shade of a forest, with the sound of tumbling water following you all the way. Rock pinnacles tower above you, and streams cascade across your path. Out of the trees, you descend to a swingbridge crossing the delightful Spasimata stream. If you thought the first half of the walk was fantastic, wait until you see this!

The walk begins at the auberge in Bonifatu (*P*15). Head up the broad forestry road, with the Figarella River below you. A thick blanket of trees covers the slopes. In **15min** a lesser track goes left across the river; go straight ahead on a path signposted for Carrozzu. Up ahead, the valley forks, and an imposing pyramid of rock splits the ravine. Snow may still linger on the peaks.

A stream is crossed at about **50min**; then, at just over **1h05min**, you cross the Ruisseau de Spasimata. This fresh limpid river must usually

98

be forded, unless you can jump from rock to rock. Over the river, your ascent becomes more noticeable. After another stream crossing you have a fine view up the valley, where a waterfall tumbles down a sheer rock face. The next stream crossing is a little awkward; wade across if you are unsure of your footing.

At **2h** you pass the remains of hillside terracing and a table and benches made of stone placed alongside the stream. A small stone shelter lies a couple of minutes further on. There is also a sign to assure you that the Refuge de Carrozzu is just 10 minutes away. Eight minutes past the signpost, another signposted junction is met. The refuge is left; Asco and the swingbridge right. First visit the wonderfully-sited refuge. You walk into a picture postcard. Over the hillside birches and pines, you have views of the lush plains far below, framed by the near-vertical valley walls. A sloping hill

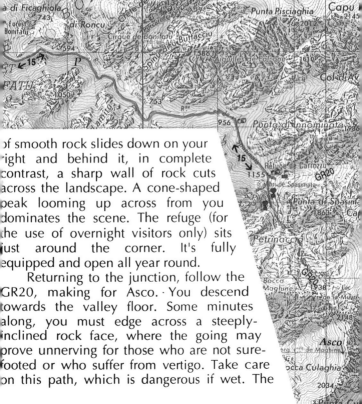

of smooth rock slides down on your right and behind it, in complete contrast, a sharp wall of rock cuts across the landscape. A cone-shaped peak looming up across from you dominates the scene. The refuge (for the use of overnight visitors only) sits just around the corner. It's fully equipped and open all year round.

Returning to the junction, follow the GR20, making for Asco. You descend towards the valley floor. Some minutes along, you must edge across a steeply-inclined rock face, where the going may prove unnerving for those who are not sure-footed or who suffer from vertigo. Take care on this path, which is dangerous if wet. The

Beyond the Spasimata swingbridge, experienced walkers can follow the GR20 towards Asco, perhaps into snow-clad terrain. This photograph was taken near the Bocca Culaghia.

Spasimata swingbridge spans the river just below you now. A cascade splashes down into a beautiful pool beneath it. This is a very exhilarating spot. A wire rope helps you down the final drop to the bridge. Crossing the bridge may give you the jitters; the only 'handrail' is a wire rope. Once over the bridge (**2h30min**), you can always wander a bit further on, following the GR20 towards Asco (see photograph above), but note that the going gets very tough. Picnicking beside the pool here is very popular 'in season'. From every angle the mountain scenery is tremendous.

Return to Bonifatu by the same route, watching your waymarkers (**4h30min**).

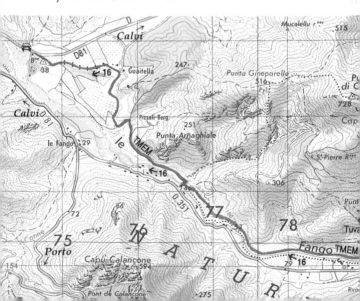

16 BONIFATU • BOCCA DI BONASSA • BOCCA DI LUCCA • TUVARELLI • GUAITELLA

Distance/time: 23km/14.3mi; 8h20min   **Map begins on pages 98-99**

Grade: strenuous climb of 650m/2130ft for the first 2h05min; the rest is a doddle ... but long. Not recommended in changeable weather. Slight possibility of vertigo.

Equipment: walking boots, sunhat, sunglasses, suncream, swimwear, long-sleeved shirt, long trousers, gloves, cardigan, anorak, raingear, picnic, water

How to get there and return: 🚌 taxi to the forestry house at Bonifatu. Arrange with the same driver to collect you at the large Guaitella camping ground on the north side of the Fango, just east of the bridge on the D81, and return via the airport — a shorter and cheaper route.

Short walks

1 Guaitella — Tuvarelli — Guaitella (easy; 3h30min). Refer to the map below and follow the orange-paint waymarking. 🚌 to and from the campsite at Guaitella (on the north side of the Fango; see map).

2 Bonifatu — Bocca di Bonassa — Bonifatu (strenuous, with a climb of 650m/2130ft, lasting 2h05min; 3h40min in all). Follow the main walk to the Bocca di Bonassa and return the same way. 🚌 as for main walk; arrange for the driver to return for you.

Huffing and puffing up to the pine woods and grassy slopes, you look out along the winding Figarella Valley to the Gulf of Calvi, before disappearing inland to a silent valley, thickly wooded in pines and oaks. At the end of this valley lies another equally as long, where the magnificent Fango River flows. If you've always preferred the sea to a river for swimming, you might just change your mind! Short walk 1 makes a perfect 'river day', as opposed to a 'beach day', and is ideal for picnicking.

From the forestry house at Bonifatu walk back downhill towards Calvi for eight minutes (see map pages 98-

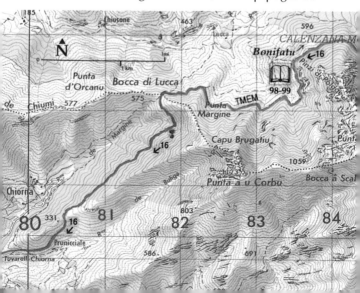

At the Bocca di Bonassa

99). **The walk starts** at the signposted footpath on your left. Orange arrows and paint daubs mark your route, which sends you climbing for the next two hours. Small streams provide good resting places en route. At **1h** ignore a turning off to the right. As you leave the woods, Calvi — just a smudge of white — and the gulf are glimpsed through the hills. Cyclamen, violets, and buttercups lie along your path, and the call of the cuckoo accompanies you. The air is alpine-fresh, and the odd fir tree enhances this atmosphere. Moss and grass cushion the hillside as you near the pass.

Close on **2h05min**, knees-a-quiver, you reach the pass, the Bocca di Bonassa (1153m/3780ft; photograph above). A dip in the distant hills reveals the Fango Valley and some scattered habitations. A very convoluted descent follows — perhaps on your backside in wet weather. *Watch your waymarking all the way from here!* The route heads downhill and then swings left (ignore animal paths branching off to the right). From a tangle of brush, a rocky nodule affords a good view down along the valley.

Near the valley floor you'll encounter oaks again; the forest is more spacious, allowing some of them to grow to a massive girth. Bouldery streambeds lie at regular intervals. Soon the way is again lit up by flowers. At about **3h50min** you cross a refreshing stream, with a line of splendid old chestnuts running down alongside it. Fifteen minutes later pass through a small chestnut grove. Don't be surprised to encounter livestock and even some wild pigs along the path. The waymarking has virtually vanished, but the level route is very obvious, and you need not watch out for any turn-off.

At **4h40min** you reach the Bocca di Lucca (575m/1885ft; see map pages 100-101) and a junction. Your direction is over the pass, to the left. Descend a side-valley that opens out into the Fango. Not far down, a stretch of path cutting across an old landslide might prove unnerving for some walkers. At **5h50min** pass through a junction and keep straight on. Tuvarelli soon appears below on the river flat. Old stone walls give it a touch of charm. Within 15 minutes you meet a rough track. Turn right along it, towards the hamlet. You approach a bridge, the Pont de Tuvarelli-Chirona (**6h 05min**). Before you continue the walk, stop and take a look at the crystal-clear pool just below it. If the weather is warm enough, you won't be able to resist jumping into this Olympic-sized waterhole. The river cuts through the rocky valley floor, leaving many lovely green-tinted rock pools along its course (**P**16).

From the bridge return to the track and then turn left onto another, narrow track, following the orange waymarks. Within three minutes you bear left on a path signposted for Galéria. Straight over the small stream, you swing back towards the river and head down alongside it. Behind you, the Monte Cinto range is streaked with streamlets of snow. At **6h45min** you come to an exquisite river setting, where diluted green-to-blue pools are set deep in a riverbed of rose-coloured, grey, and mauve rock. Time for another dip? Thirty-five minutes from the pools (**7h20min**) the path comes out onto the track crossing the bridge shown below. Beneath this beautiful arched bridge lies another irre-

sistible swimming spot. After your swim, head right (north) along the track, then take the first turn-off left (a narrow dirt track). Pass a faint fork off to the right and, at a junction (Guaitella) 15 minutes later (**8h**), bear left. At **8h20min** meet the Calvi road, the D81.

This beautiful arched bridge near Guaitella is on the route of both the main walk and Short walk 1.

17 BARGHIANA • BOCCA DI CAPRONALE • BARGHIANA

Distance/time: 20.5km/12.75mi; 9h20min

Grade: long, and very strenuous, with a climb of 1160m/3800ft. Cold and dangerous in bad weather. Possibility of vertigo — *and of landslides. Only recommended for experienced and hardy hikers.*

Equipment: walking boots, sunhat, sunglasses, suncream, long-sleeved shirt, long trousers, gloves, cardigan, warm jacket, raingear, picnic, water, swimwear

How to get there and return: 🚗 hired car (Barghiana is 41.5km from Calvi, via the airport route).

Short walk: from Barghiana to the end of the track (where a small foot-bridge crosses a cascading stream), and return. Easy; 4h20min.

The rewards for this walk will cost you dearly, so save the next day for the beach! This unfrequented, *and unwaymarked* footpath climbs through a pleasant evergreen oak forest, following an old mule trail to the Niolo Plateau. Out of the woods, you come to the end of the valley and find that you're completely walled in! Sheer mountainsides tower above you. But your spectacular onward trail takes you up and over these walls, along precipitous ledges. In all my hiking on Corsica, only on these summits have I spotted the rare moufflon, but I have to confess it's usually only their bums, as they vanish amidst the rock. Good luck!

Leave your transport by the cemetery just outside Barghiana, where the road descends to cross the river. **The walk begins** on the lower track that leaves from the lay-by here. Straightaway you look up at towering peaks. Monte Estremo is the hamlet of stone dwellings strung out along the sheer hillside opposite. The Fango (Walk 16) flows below you. Soon the Capu Tafunatu (2335m/7660ft) catches your eye. A gaping hole the size of a tennis court pierces the peak. One tale tells of

the devil who, boasting of his powers to St Martin, attempted to build a bridge over the torrents of the Golo in a single night. All was complete bar the keystone, when a shepherd in prayer disturbed a nearby cock, causing it to crow. In a fit of rage, the devil hurled his hammer in the air. It flew straight through the Capu Tafunatu,

View across the valley, 1h into the walk

104

landing just off the west coast and thus forming the Girolata Gulf ...

The valley forks, and a small pastoral outpost is seen sitting in the gentle slope below, shaded by chestnut trees. Beyond a stone bridge (the Ponte di e Rocce) you look straight onto the barrier of mountains that make up the red-hued Cinto range. At about **2h** the track narrows to a path and a gushing stream is crossed. The Short walk ends at this delightful spot.

The main walk continues up the path, after about 30 minutes passing the remains of the old canton house, set back in the trees above the track, just beyond a small bubbly stream. Animal tracks make the route a bit confusing, but there *is* one main mule trail. Pass a spring on your left 15 minutes up from the canton house. The valley terminates in sheer curving walls just up ahead. Crossing the valley floor, you get a view back onto the rose-coloured hills. And then the climb begins. The path ascends in sweeping zigzags, frequently interrupted by animal paths cutting straight up the sides of the slopes. Stretches of scree (unnerving for inexperienced hikers) will slow you up. It's more than likely, too, that you'll have to squeeze past timid cows and calves grazing the narrow ledges. Please go *very quietly,* and give them 'right of way'.

At **5h** you reach the pass (Bocca di Capronale; 1329m/4360ft). The prominent peak to the north is the Punta Silvareccia (1964m/6440ft). The path continues round the valley to the Niolo. As lovely as this vista may be, your eyes will always return to those red hills.

From here return the same way to Barghiana (**9h 20min**). Take the steep, gravelly descent slowly. If it's not too late when you return, how about a dip in one of the Fango's inviting rock pools?

105

18 GALERIA • PUNTA DI A LITERNICCIA • GIROLATA • D81

Distance/time: 17km/10.5mi; 6h40min

Grade: long and strenuous, with a climb lasting 2h30min near the start. Overall ascent 740m/2430ft. Possibility of vertigo. Waymarking at times hard to follow. Not recommended in changeable weather.

Equipment: walking boots, sunhat, sunglasses, suncream, long trousers, long-sleeved shirt, swimwear, cardigan, anorak, raingear, picnic, water

How to get there: ⛴ to Galéria (Timetable 11). The Christophe Colombe is the only boat stopping there; *moreover, always verify departures the day before you set out!*

To return: 🚌 Arrange for someone to meet you at the end of the walk (on the D81, south of the Palmarella Pass; see map). Alternatively, end the walk at Girolata and take the ⛴ to Calvi (Timetable 11). This does not leave time to enjoy the walk however — only time enough to rush through it! Try to stay overnight at Girolata (accommodation in simple huts (telephone 95.20.15.43), a *gîte* (similar to a youth hostel; take your own sleeping bags), or one of the inns (telephone 95.26.10.98 or 95.20.16.98). In high season book well in advance.

Short walk: Bocca a Croce — Girolata — Bocca a Croce (moderate; 3h20min). *Don't miss this walk!* Start out from the parking area at the Bocca a Croce (🚌 to go and return). The path begins its descent just below the road. Pass a fountain in 15min. Near the Plage de Taura, just before a sturdy stone wall bordering the path, turn off the path and drop down to the streambed and beach (40min). Continue alongside another wall and cross the streambed. Re-enter scrub and meet a junction. Keep left and straight up. In 25min a path joins you from the right. Keep straight on over the ridge and descend to Girolata (25min downhill; 1h30min). The best time to arrive is before 11.30 or after 14.00, when the excursion boats are not there. Return the same way.

The invigorating boat journey to Galéria makes this walk unique on Corsica. (It can be a little choppy, so hopefully you have 'sea legs'!) From the port of Calvi superb coastal scenery follows you all the way, from the citadel, via the red cliffs of the Punta Scandola and the maquis-wooded hills that slip off into the sea, to the sheer mountains of granite bursting up out of the Girolata Gulf. Girolata is a beautifully-sited, rustic tourist-trap only accessible by boat or on foot. Excursion boats disgorge day-trippers here for a two-hour lunch before returning. However, once the tourists have gone, peace reigns again, and the natural beauty of this tiny fishing port can be really appreciated.

When the boat has run aground (intentionally) and you have climbed down the ladder and onto the beach at Galéria, **the walk begins**. Head along the beach over to the restaurant on your right. Follow the road behind it into the village. Minutes along, just after crossing a bridge, you come to two roads forking off to the right.

Climb the second of them. A few minutes up, you're in the centre of Galéria, at an intersection. Here there is still some 'character', but the rest of the place is a touristic hodge-podge. Its splendid beach and the bay it sits behind are the main assets of this small resort. Bear right at the intersection and remain on this road for the next 15 minutes. Some 200m/yds over a bridge, take the path forking to the left. It's well marked with signposts and orange paint. Stone walls flank your route briefly, before it disappears into woods. Fifteen minutes along you encounter two forks, a minute apart: keep right at the first and left at the second.

Just over the valley floor you rise to a junction. Your way is to the right, and you pass above a muddy reservoir cradled in the valley floor (**50min**). The cacophony of chorusing frogs is almost deafening. Fifteen minutes from the reservoir, you begin a series of stream crossings over the Tavulaghiu. Trees draped with vines and creepers shade the way. The ascent begins, up into the high surrounding hills. At about **1h55min** a balcony of rock makes a good viewpoint: you have uninterrupted vistas over the Galéria Gulf and the neighbouring bay. Galéria itself sits back off the shore. The slope is covered in junipers, and in early summer the last of the thorny broom florets add their cheerful colour and delightful fragrance.

Fifteen minutes uphill from the viewpoint, you mount the summit of this bumpy ridge and begin to descend along it, accompanied by views to the central massif. Monte Cinto (2706m/8875ft), the island's highest peak, stands head and shoulders above the rest. A brief climb follows, up to a grassy flat area (the Punta di a Literniccia; **2h20min**), lightly wooded in holm oaks. Go right at the fork here, remaining on the crest of the ridge. (A left turn leads to the main road and the Palmarella Pass.)

Soon the Girolata Gulf comes into sight far below. This exquisite setting is dramatised by a twin-breasted sheer mountain (Monte Seninu, 619m/2030ft) that rears

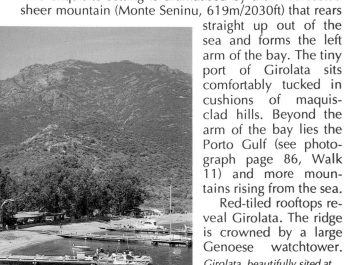

straight up out of the sea and forms the left arm of the bay. The tiny port of Girolata sits comfortably tucked in cushions of maquis-clad hills. Beyond the arm of the bay lies the Porto Gulf (see photograph page 86, Walk 11) and more mountains rising from the sea.

Red-tiled rooftops reveal Girolata. The ridge is crowned by a large Genoese watchtower.

Girolata, beautifully sited at the foot of scrub-covered hills

Clambering along the crest becomes rather awkward and slow-going. Watch your footing; it's very rocky, and the cliffs drop away quite steeply in places. You go from waymarking dot to waymarking dot, weaving in and out of thorny broom. More wonderful seascapes follow, this time to your right.

At about **3h20min**, immediately below an antenna, the path veers over to the right flank of the ridge. The waymarking becomes difficult to follow, as you remount the ridge and descend it again. Roughly 15 minutes below the antenna, the path swings back on itself: the main path appears to go off to the left here, but in fact loops back sharply to the right to cross the crest yet again.

At about **3h45min** pass through a clearing and go by the remains of a stone building with a nearby wheat-threshing floor. From here the path descends to the left of the Capu Licchia, down a lateral ridge. The turquoise Girolata Gulf becomes brighter as you descend. Heading down a crest, meet a fork (**4h25min**). Bear right here and cross over the crest, to descend into a small side valley. Leaving this valley, you look across the bay to majestic Mount Seninu. The jagged pink and mauve headland of the Punta Scandola, on your right, holds your attention with its rich colouring.

Coming into Girolata (**5h**), you step down through a small cluster of modest pink stone dwellings. The prominent remains of the tower dominate the cove. A few wooden sheds, a lean-to restaurant/bar, and even a stable sit in the shade of scruffy eucalyptus trees around the cove, enhancing the 'out-in-the-sticks' appeal of this hamlet. The wooden jetties and handful of yachts hint at tourism, but all is quiet before 11.30 or after 14.00. If you enjoy lobster, this is the place to tuck in; Girolata's *other* income derives from lobster-fishing.

Moving on, the same day or the next, pick up your continuation at the other end of the beach. Glorious views follow you all the way uphill. A tiring ascent takes you up to the Calvi/Porto road (be sure to turn off left at the junction 35 minutes up; straight ahead is the way to the Plage de Tuara on the Short walk route). Reach the D81 some 2km south of the Col de Palma-rella (**6h40min**). *Attention:* No signs mark the point where the path joins the road but, by referring to the walking map, you can arrange to meet at the deep curve in the road (where the height is shown as 352m).

19 POZZO • BOCCA DI SANTA MARIA • MONTE STELLO • POZZO

Distance/time: 6km/3.75mi; 5h15min

Grade: strenuous, with an ascent of 1080m/3540ft. Recommended for experienced mountain walkers *only*. Don't attempt in changeable weather, and *don't forget your spectacles:* the waymarking is very hard to follow!

Equipment: walking boots, sunhat, sunglasses, suncream, long-sleeved shirt, long trousers, cardigan, anorak, raingear, picnic, water

How to get there: 🚌 to Lavasina (Timetable 14), then follow the Short walk up to Pozzo (add 1h05min); or 🚗 taxi from Bastia to Pozzo
To return: by taxi or bus, as above

Short walk: Lavasina — Poretto — Pozzo — Lavasina (strenuous, but short, with a steep climb of 277m/910ft on good paths; 1h50min). 🚌 to Lavasina (Timetable 14). Head straight up the lane to the left of the church in Lavasina. 3min uphill, continue on the path. Minutes later follow the right-hand driveway in front of you. Climb it until you meet and cross the road, then continue on a mule track. Keep right at the T-junction; you're soon in Poretto, on a driveway. Some 35m/yds uphill, bear right along a lane and, within a minute, turn up the steps on your left. Cross a lane and, metres/yards further up, take the first right-hand turn between the houses. Come to the church and remain above it; then, when the lane swings right, leave it to continue on a path. Pass steps climbing to the left and then an impressive fountain. Soon you reach the road, where you turn right downhill. Some 80m/yds down, fork left up a concrete lane. When it ends, pass a garage on your left (prepare yourself for the dogs here), and follow the path leading uphill between high stone walls. You come out alongside a church. Continue along the alley towards the door of the convent shown below, but climb the steps on the left just before reaching it. Cross a road and continue briefly on a mule track. Meet the Pozzo road and go left to the village square (1h05min). Return the same way.

Monte Stello (1307m/4290ft), the highest mountain on Cap Corse, offers you the best views possible over this strange finger of schist rock. But, there *is* one catch. Monte Stello is not very generous in sharing this

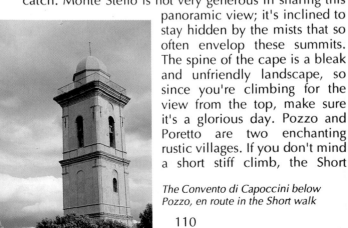

panoramic view; it's inclined to stay hidden by the mists that so often envelop these summits. The spine of the cape is a bleak and unfriendly landscape, so since you're climbing for the view from the top, make sure it's a glorious day. Pozzo and Poretto are two enchanting rustic villages. If you don't mind a short stiff climb, the Short

The Convento di Capoccini below Pozzo, en route in the Short walk

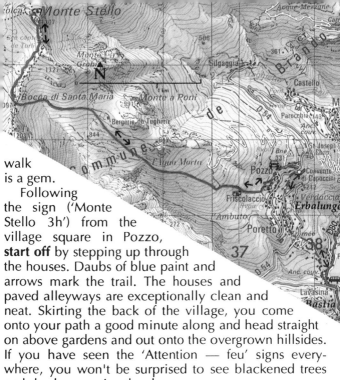

walk
is a gem.

Following the sign ('Monte Stello 3h') from the village square in Pozzo, **start off** by stepping up through the houses. Daubs of blue paint and arrows mark the trail. The houses and paved alleyways are exceptionally clean and neat. Skirting the back of the village, you come onto your path a good minute along and head straight on above gardens and out onto the overgrown hillsides. If you have seen the 'Attention — feu' signs every-where, you won't be surprised to see blackened trees and shrubs covering the slopes.

Cross a streambed **3min** up, then edge your way along a terrace wall. *It's slippery and crumbling — take care!* Almost at once you have a problem: which path should you follow? There are several. Remember, as long as you're following *some* kind of waymarking, whether it be red, blue or white paint, as well as small piles of stones, you'll reach the summit. I found the white paint waymarks easiest to follow: on this route you will pass a derelict stone cottage in **15min**. Go through a stone wall just beyond it and, eight minutes further up, pass below the remains of another stone building. You should gradually be veering over to the left, towards a valley that cuts back into the flank of this ridge. Eventually you enter this valley.

Within **1h40min** you climb past a delicious spring (it lies just beyond a water tank), to reach the Bergerie de Teghime sheltering against an outcrop of rock. This is a pleasant spot to get your breath back and quench your thirst before the final assault. From here up, a sharp eye is needed to follow the piles of stones and the less frequent daubs of white paint, both of which are obscured by the maquis. Your continuation heads off between the two fenced-off enclosures at the *bergerie*.

111

Bastia: approaching from the south on the N193.

The path divides as it ascends toward a pass (the Bocca di Santa Maria). The way to the left is easier to follow, but don't cross the V in the hillside.

Approaching **2h30min** you cross the pass and over-look a reclining, bowl-shaped valley and the small village of Piazza, well concealed from the coast. Over a shimmering, blue bay (the Golfe de Sant-Florent) you see the outlines of the arid hills of the Désert des Agriates. As you cross over the back of the ridge, Monte Stello, a sprawling rocky hill rising out of this backbone of schist, appears to the right … adorned with an antenna of sorts. A couple of minutes downhill to the right you should pick up a trail: *set up waymarkers exactly where you join it,* so that you leave it at the same place on your return. Another pass lies between this one and Monte Stello and, on the return, it's easy to mistake that pass for your turn-off point.

On rounding the back of the ridge keep near the crest. About 15 minutes over the pass, a rock with an arrow and '500m' painted on it marks your final ascent. Either take the easier, longer path to the left (it approaches the summit from behind), or follow the white waymarkers and scramble straight up (right) over rock. At **3h** you're at the top, the best viewing point over the cape. Bare rocky hills topple off this wavy mountain range, rolling off into the sea on either side of you. On the clearest days your view stretches to the island's summits. To the east and not far below lie the scattered villages of Sisco (swallowed up in greenery) and (further along the coast) Marine de Pietracorbara.

The return requires attention at two places: where you turn off to cross the pass, and just over the pass, where it's not easy to find the continuation. Here, keep down near the V in the hillside, until you find some waymarking. End the day by popping in to the very friendly, family-run café in Pozzo's square (**5h15min**).

See also photograph page 27

Distance/time: 17.5km/11mi; 6h20min

Grade: fairly strenuous, with a climb of 400m/1310ft. For about 1h beyond Tralonca, the path is slightly overgrown and hard to follow. Some clambering over fences, gates, and rock walls. Slippery in wet weather; possibility of vertigo.

Equipment: walking boots, sunhat, suncream, sunglasses, long-sleeved shirt, long trousers, cardigan, anorak, raingear, picnic, water, and spectacles, if you wear them!

How to get there: to Corte (Timetable 21)
To return: same train

There are no high passes on this walk, which is accessible to all sturdy hill walkers. A magnificent backdrop of mountain scenery encircles you throughout, but you'll see golden hayfields lining quiet valley floors and grassy slopes *not* dominated by rock. You'll enjoy making the acquaintance of two delightful villages, too — Santa-Lucia-di-Mercurio, recently revived, and the brilliantly-perched Tralonca.

Leaving the train in Corte, **start the walk** by bearing right from the station exit and crossing the Tavignano River. Come to the D39, the first *main* road off right. Turn along it. From here on dashes of orange paint mark your route. Follow *only* these orange dashes; ignore the other waymarking for the moment. At around **8min**, fork left on a gravel track signposted 'Sentiers du Boziu' and 'Santa Lucia'. Barely a minute up this track, bear right on a mule track running alongside a fence (on the other side of which lives a noisy dog). Some 25 minutes from the station you cross over low hills, pass through an intersection, and descend into the gentle open valley of hayfields. At a fork minutes later, keep left. Steep grassy slopes rise back off the valley; these are dominated by Monte Tomboni (1061m/3480ft). Large hawks fly up out of the fields when they spot your approach. Bear left at the fork just before an abandoned farm building.

Descending to the valley floor, you reach a stream and bear right alongside it, following the orange paint. A minute along you cross this alder-shaded stream. Back on the mule track, soon clamber over a fence and continue straight on. Barely eight minutes across the stream, confront a junction of paths. Climb up left and, almost immediately, when the path forks, keep left again. Three minutes further up you cross the railway lines (**55min**), to walk alongside, *but not join* a path or your right. Eyes glued to the waymarking, loop your way up the thistle-covered hillside, where small flocks of sheep graze. As you climb, look back at the superb country scenery unravelling behind you: a barrier of mountains rises up behind Corte, with great valleys slicing back into them: from left to right the Restonica, the Tavignano, and the Asco.

At **1h15min** come to a small flat area and pass through vestiges of stone walls. Within the next 15 minutes, you'll cross two muddy streamlets, crammed with ferns. Corte becomes the focal point in the landscape, its apartment blocks dwarfed by the strong backdrop of mountains. You, meanwhile, are carefully making your way from rock to rock, looking out for the splashes of paint. Patches of tall, majestic Scottish thistles lie scattered across the inclines. In summer the ground moves with grasshoppers, so climb with your mouth closed!

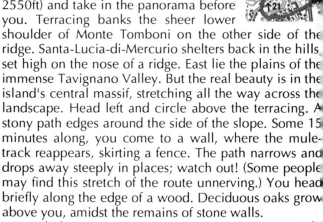

Close on **1h50min** you drag yourself over a pass, the Bocca di Civenti (777m/ 2550ft) and take in the panorama before you. Terracing banks the sheer lower shoulder of Monte Tomboni on the other side of the ridge. Santa-Lucia-di-Mercurio shelters back in the hills, set high on the nose of a ridge. East lie the plains of the immense Tavignano Valley. But the real beauty is in the island's central massif, stretching all the way across the landscape. Head left and circle above the terracing. A stony path edges around the side of the slope. Some 15 minutes along, you come to a wall, where the mule-track reappears, skirting a fence. The path narrows and drops away steeply in places; watch out! (Some people may find this stretch of the route unnerving.) You head briefly along the edge of a wood. Deciduous oaks grow above you, amidst the remains of stone walls.

Just below Santa-Lucia meet a junction: turn right and cross a stream. Beyond some neat stone buildings scramble over a gate to meet a track. Climb it. (Signs for Corte/Tralonca stand by the track, but this old route to Tralonca is impassable.) Continue up the road into Santa-Lucia. Pass the old washing-place (on your right) and head up the lovely cobbled path to the square at the top of the village (**3h**). Creepers cling to walls, and the houses are shuttered — all the charm of a sleepy

village.
While the surrounding terrain is overgrown, Santa-Lucia commands magnificent views. Making for Tralonca, take the bumpy country road out of the village (keeping the water fountain on your right). Ignore the branch-off left three minutes along. Winding through a narrow valley, you continue circling Monte Tromboni.

Soon strategically-sited Tralonca interrupts the landscape. A background of mountains enhances its fine setting. When you reach the village (**3h50min**), do it justice and climb up into it. After your visit, walk down the main road for about 200m/yds, until you see a sign denoting the exit for Tralonca. Here turn off down a path into the valley below. This stretch of the hike is not waymarked, so prepare to lose some time getting lost. You come to the setting shown on page 27. Proud old stone walls, in varying stages of decay, flank your way. Gulleys tumble away on either side of you. Nearing the end of the ridge, barely eight minutes beyond the stone house in the photograph, the path swings sharp right. Your turning point is just beyond a low crumbled wall. Zigzagging down the right-hand flank of the ridge through kermes oak, you follow a frayed path that takes you around the nose of a ridge where you pass above a derelict building (eight minutes after passing through the crumbled wall). Here the path swings around the nose of the ridge into the valley on your left. You are following the remains of the old muleteers' route, which in places is quite overgrown.

Immediately beyond the ruins of a third building (near the valley floor), turn sharp right and head straight towards the stream. Just under 35 minutes from Tralonca, cross the stream and pick up a clear path below another stone building. You disappear into a dense coppice, following a cow-trail. The path braids itself and at times is confusing; just remain near the floor of the valley. Ignore a path joining from the left. Approaching **4h35min**, cross a glade and rejoin the path at the opposite end of it (near some crumbled buildings). At the fork that follows, keep on the upper path, rounding the hillside. Ten minutes beyond the glade you'll see a large farm-shed across the floor of the valley. At about this point, red and yellow, and red and white tape on shrubs and bushes alert you to a fork on your right. It descends to the valley floor. Ignore it; keep straight on (the left-hand fork) around the hillside, following these same strips of tape. A minute from the fork pass through a gate.

At around **5h05min** the path forks; follow the tape to the left. Eight minutes later pass above another derelict building. A small copse of kermes oak follows, and soon you're not far above the railway. Keep right at the fork you encounter just over a dry streambed (above the railway). You rejoin your outbound route at **5h40min**, just above where you first crossed the railway. Heading back across it, bear left, and once again follow the orange paint waymarking (*not* the tape). In 40 minutes you're back at Corte's station (**6h20min**).

Tralonca sits like a gabled roof-top, high on a pointed hillock. You'll be surprised at how many houses have been crammed onto this outcrop. A pleasant fountain and washing place are opposite the church.

21 CORTE • GORGES DU TAVIGNANO • REFUGE DE SEGA • CORTE

Distance/time: 32.5km/20.25mi; 11h40min   **Photograph page 30**

Grade: very strenuous and very long, with total ascent of 1172m/ 3845ft. Only suitable for fit and experienced hikers. Can be very cold and wet; don't attempt in uncertain weather. Danger of vertigo. *This walk is best done in two days,* with an overnight stay at the Refuge de Sega. Take a sleeping-bag and food; cooking gas is provided. Unfortunately, you *cannot reserve a place in advance* (no telephone).

Equipment: walking boots, sunhat, sunglasses, suncream, swimwear, long trousers, long-sleeved shirt, gloves cardigan, warm jacket, raingear, picnic, water

How to get there: 🚆 to Corte (Timetable 21)
To return: same train

Shorter walk: to the swingbridge at the 2h30min-point in the main walk and return (moderate; 5h).

In summer, the most memorable feature of this walk is the lake-sized pool that sits behind the Refuge de Sega (photograph page 30). Tearing yourself away from it is almost impossible; everyone makes a mad dash to catch the last train. Before you reach the refuge, you wind up a gorge, dwarfed by lofty rock walls. Below you lie other pools, inaccessible but tantalisingly beautiful.

Begin the walk at Corte's railway station: head left and make for the town centre. Cross the Restonica and Tavignano rivers. Immediately beyond the Tavignano (**15min**), turn left up a road that circles behind the town (it follows the Tavignano), and follow the daubs of orange paint. The old citadel crowns the hilltop above in a precarious fashion. Close on **35min**, leave the road (on a bend), turning left on a signposted gravel track. Some 55m/yds along, fork left on a waymarked path, and climb into the valley. Two minutes in, come to a fork and scramble up right, soon circling some hillside terracing. At **1h05min** the path forks three ways: take either of the top two branches. The riverbed is a string of beryl-green pools. The valley narrows, and the landscape becomes more dramatic, with rocky salients piercing the pine-studded walls. Come to a prominent rock belvedere that bulges out of the wall high above the river at **1h50min**. Forty minutes later (**2h30min**) cross the Tavignano on a swingbridge. The Shorter walk ends at this scenic spot; cool off and enjoy a picnic.

Over the bridge your continuation veers slightly left at first, before turning right above the river. An arduous ascent follows, through a well-wooded hillside. Looking through the trees onto bare rocky summits, you'll notice a thin veil of green lichen covering these heights.

The impressive dome of the Capu Aleri (1634m/5360ft) stands out at the right of the valley. Fifty minutes above the swingbridge you encounter a 15-minute stretch of path which is both awkward and vertiginous. Take special care here if it's wet underfoot. Ignore the faint fork to the left barely five minutes over the streambed (**3h35min**). If you meet any livestock on the narrow ledges, skirt them quietly — or move them on quietly, until you can pass. *Don't frighten them!*

A tiny reservoir in the river below catches your eye. It looks inviting but is shallow. A better pool lies just below it. From here on the way evens out, and the valley floor is wider. Passing through moss- and lichen-covered rock you come upon the Refuge de Sega — a stone 'Hansel and Gretel' cottage set amidst pines below the path (**4h50min**). Behind the refuge is the pool shown on page 30, an exquisite beauty spot.

Continue the walk by heading past the refuge; you cross the river on another swingbridge. Off the bridge bear right. Follow the orange-paint waymarks; there's no clear path for the first several minutes. You pass below a bare granite hillside and come to a stream. Cross it and, a good minute later, climb past a lovely waterfall. Orange dashes guide you up through a profusion of lily-like sea daffodils (*Pancratium maritimum*).

Some 1h05min from the refuge you pass alongside the Bergerie de Boniacce (**5h55min**), a shepherds' outpost with a spring at the left of the buildings. Bear left on the track just above the *bergerie*, and rejoin your path some 80m/yds uphill, on the right. Cross another track eight minutes later. In another eight minutes (**6h 10min**), just over the Bocca a l'Arinella, an unsurpassed sight greets you — a sweeping view over the immense Golo Valley and across the 'kingdom' of the Niolo, an isolated and very traditional region of Corsica.

Home is all downhill. Return to the last track you crossed and follow it to the left. Ignore the fork 15min along. You pass the Refuge Melo at **6h45min**. Some 1h05min along the track (**7h20min**) *watch for your turn-off:* head left off a sharp bend to the right. (A pine with a blue arrow stands at the turn-off. If you come to a sign 'Chantier interdit au public', you have gone too far.) Your narrow path leads you into a magnificent forest of towering *Laricio* pines, the Forêt Dominiale du Tavignano. Your only waymarking will be a few small piles of stones. In minutes you cross two small streams.

Keep right, round the hillside. Pass a left fork within ten minutes and, 25 minutes later, just beyond an abandoned forestry house, you will be back on the track. If your flask needs refilling, head *right* along the track for a couple of minutes, to the Funtana d'Argento; otherwise go *left* for a few metres/yards, to pick up the continuing path on your right; it's rough and somewhat overgrown. This descent back into the Tavignano Valley requires a lot of concentration.

At about **9h10min** you rejoin your outgoing route at the first swingbridge and head straight back to Corte, 2h 30min away (**11h40min**).

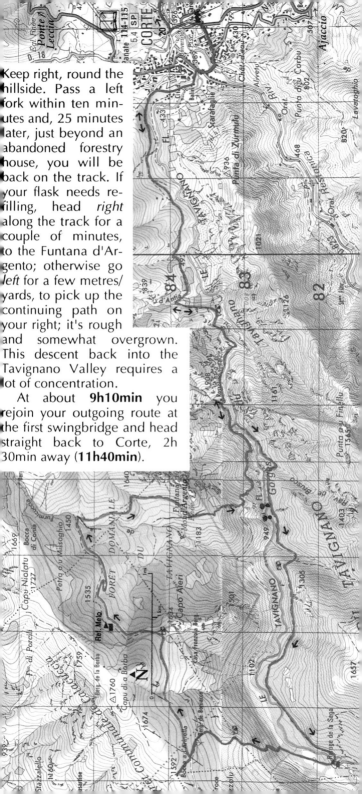

22 BERGERIE DE GROTTELLE • LAC DE MELU • LAC DU CAPITELLU • BERGERIE DE GROTTELLE

Distance/time: 6km/3.75mi; 3h35min

Grade: strenuous but short (with a steep climb of 560m/1835ft). Very dangerous if wet. Can be very cold; don't attempt in unpredictable weather. There are two routes up to the lakes (see text below).

Equipment: walking boots, sunhat, suncream, sunglasses, swimwear, long-sleeved shirt, long trousers, cardigan, warm jacket, gloves, raingear, picnic, water

How to get there and return: 🚐 car or taxi to the Bergerie de Grottelle (D623, 15km from Corte). For trains to Corte see Timetable 21.

Shorter walk: Bergerie de Grottelle — Lac de Melu — Bergerie de Grottelle (fairly strenuous; 2h45min). Take the easier route (see below).

Whether you are a walker or not, do make the effort to see the Lac de Melu. It's picture-postcard-perfect. The whole Restonica Valley is a wealth of superb scenery, with overpowering peaks, cascading streams, and spell-binding glacial lakes. The aching muscles may not be so memorable, but your photographs surely will.

The well-trodden path **sets off** from the car park at Bergerie de Grottelle at the top of the D623 and is signposted 'Melu/Capitellu'. Yellow paint marks the route. At the outset, you look straight up at the Capu a Chiostru (2295m/7530ft). It rises abruptly in front of you on the right. On your left stands the impenetrable Rotondo Massif. Bright green patches of alders illuminate the rocky inclines. Thorny broom and foxgloves keep you company, as does the racket of streams crashing down the mountainsides.

Some **25min** up (eight minutes after crossing two streams metres/yards apart), the easier path forks off left, across a grassy patch (*P*22). (*Less experienced walkers should use this path.* Watch for the yellow paint and small piles of stones, just inside the fork; you cross the Restonica immediately. The turn-off itself is a bit hard to find, but the rest of the way is very straightforward.)

Mountaineers can follow the more difficult route, up over the bare rock. Soon you're crawling — *keep both*

On the N193 making for Corte: rainbows frequently play above the landscape in spring and autumn.

The Lac de Melu

hands free! Not long before mounting the saddle, you will have to haul yourself up with chains (**50min**). Clambering over the last of the rock, you cross the pass and straight in front of you find an amphitheatre of rock. A few steps further on, you're at the Lac de Melu — a dark green mirror filling the basin floor. Across the lake lies the perfect picnic spot, a gentle grassy slope shaded by alders. The short walk ends here. Lap up the sun …

The Lac du Capitellu lies just above the cascading stream you can see on the right-hand side of the mountain walls. Re-locate the yellow paint and climb straight up the steep mountainside. Remain on the right-hand side of the stream for the first 25 minutes. Crossing the stream is a little tricky, and an 'all-fours' climb follows. A little over 35 minutes up from the Lac de Melu (**1h50min**), perhaps red in the face, you squeeze through a gap in the hillside to find Lake Capitellu, an indigo-blue pool ensconced in a 40m/130ft-deep hollow in the mountainside. The Capu a i Sorbi (2267m/7435ft) leans back off it to your right. You can sit here for hours getting drunk on the intoxicating scenery.

Returning is much easier. Take the other route downhill: cross the stream at the Lac de Melu and descend beside the right-hand wall of the valley. Thirty-five minutes down from Melu, go left at the fork just before the Restonica and cross the stream, to join the main path back to the bergerie (**3h35min**).

23 BAVELLA • FOCE FINOSA • REFUGE DE PALIRI • BAVELLA

Distance/time: 8km/5mi; 4h

Grade: fairly strenuous, but could be done by anyone agile. Short steep, rocky ascents totalling about 200m/655ft. Don't attempt i changeable weather. Dangerous if wet.

Equipment: walking boots, sunhat, sunglasses, suncream, gloves long-sleeved shirt, long trousers, warm jacket, cardigans, anorak raingear, picnic, water

How to get there: 🚌 to Bavella (Timetable 5), *in season only and vi the inland route*; otherwise 🚗 rental car
To return: same bus or car

Short walk: Bavella — Foce Finosa — Bavella (moderate-strenuous 2h30min). Follow the main walk for the first 1h15min; then return.

T he Massif of Bavella, with its towering pink walls o jutting crags and magnificent pine forest, has a magnetic beauty that even non-walkers will find hard to resist. And then there are the views … some of the finest on Corsica. On the grassy, cushion-soft incline that hide amidst the rock, no picnic has ever tasted more delicious.

Start out by following the track that heads off to the right of the Auberge du Col de Bavella; the first few metres are tarred. From the outset you have a superb view that stretches to the sea, but it's the formidable wall of rocky pink crags bulging out of the landscape and blocking your way that holds your attention (**P**23) Pines wood the sheer slopes. Your waymarking is the red and white paint of the GR20. From here the modes settlement of Bavella is concealed by woods. Some **25min** along, leave the track: fork left on a path (there i a path forking off to the right just before this turning). A steep descent takes you down into a wooded gulley The inclines are spongy with grass and patched with fern, the pines elegantly tall and straight (**P**23).

Just over **40min** en route, you drop down onto another track. Turn right along it. Pass a fork off to the right and soon cross an ebullient stream (you may have to wade across in springtime). Minutes over the ford, a signpost for the Refuge de Paliri directs you up a path to the right. Zigzag up the steep rocky path to the summit and the *col* (pass), the Foce Finosa (1206m/3960ft **1h15min**). The Short walk turns back here.

From the very start of the walk, the formidable wall of rocky pink crags bulging out of the landscape captures your attention.

To enjoy the best views you need to scramble (*with great care*) up onto the crest of the ridge above this pass, so that you can see over the pines. The awe-inspiring Bavella Massif rises inland: massive slabs of rock lining the valley walls dominate the landscape. On the coast lies the Golfe de Porto-Vecchio with its scooped-out, white-collared bays. In your immediate surroundings, the rock can be anything from a soft pink to a deep rose, depending on the time of day.

Continuing on to the Refuge de Paliri, descend the very steep and rocky hill below the pass, looking straight across to the magnificent Porto-Vecchio Gulf. Fortunately, this jarring descent changes direction and swings left across the flank of the ridge, to meet a junction 35 minutes below the pass. Your new route (the GR20) veers up left, as indicated by an arrow.

Around **2h** into the hike, you cross two streams close together (you can fill your canteens), just below the Refuge de Paliri. This small alpine retreat comes as a pleasant surprise. Built of stone and with a wooden roof, it could be an up-market shepherds' hut. It shelters amongst rock on a grassy slope, and in the company of a few splendid pines dwarfed by the backdrop of great granite cliffs.

Picnickers, you have a choice of two spots, either at the wooden table and benches below the hut, or just over the rocky crest to the right of the refuge, where there is another, more sheltered, picnic site. When you've tired of this blissfully peaceful spot, return to Bavella the way you came (**4h**).

24 CASCADE DE PISCIA DI GALLO

Distance/time: 2.5km/1.5mi; 1h20min

Grade: easy until you reach the gorge, then a very awkward, steep descent lasting 7min follows, down into the gorge. But it is not necessary to descend into the gorge; you can see the top half of the waterfall from the edge. The descent into the gorge is dangerous in wet weather. Total descent/ascent of 120m/400ft.

Equipment: walking shoes/boots with good grip, sunhat, sunglasses, suncream, swimwear, long trousers, long-sleeved shirt, gloves, cardigan, warm jacket, rainwear, picnic, water

How to get there: 🚌 car or taxi to the snack bar La Cascada on the D368. Or 🚐 to the snack bar La Cascada, at the turn-off to the Piscia di Gallo (Timetable 5; *July and August only*).
To return: 🚌 or the same bus

T he Piscia di Gallo waterfall is more striking for its setting than its size, although it does fall 50m/165ft in one sheer drop, shooting straight out of a sheer face of rock. To me the setting is reminiscent of the Orient: a mountain scene painted by a Chinese master.

The bus will drop you at the snack bar La Cascada. It's also the best place to park your car. Either **start the walk** by taking the path that heads off from the two snack bars here, or head east along the road for 100m/ yds and turn down the track forking off to the left (where there is a small sign, 'Cascada').

Picnic 24:
The Cascade de Piscia di Gallo shoots straight down a sheer rock face in a setting reminiscent of an oriental watercolour.

This track, marked with red arrows and dots, takes you down through a forest of young pines. Less than **15min** down, just after crossing a small stream, the track veers off left. You, however, follow the path off to the right, as the waymarking indicates. A minute later you have to wade across a wide stream. Or, if your balance is good, try hopping across the wobbly stepping-stones. Over the stream, follow the path off to the right, climbing a rocky surface. You reach a low crest, from where you bear left. (A path forks off right here, down to another stream, the Ruisseau di Piscia di Gallo, the source of the waterfall. It's a quiet 'away from it all' setting, if you're already in a picnic mood; *P*24.)

A bouldery landscape with heather and pines lies before you. Further along the ridge, you can see a stretch of coastline. Close on **20min** pass another fork, this one off to the left. In the rocky gulley below you on the right is the Ruisseau de Piscia di Gallo; it seems surprisingly small, bearing in mind the size of the waterfall it becomes. Your way heads across the rock and through the maquis. Watch the waymarking, as livestock paths also cross the path you are following.

Just before the main descent you come face to face with some enormous boulders. Here the path turns sharp right and, as you begin the descent, the top half of the waterfall comes into sight (**30min**; *P*24). It leaps out of a towering rock face and plummets into a gorge of dense vegetation. An impressive sight, but even more so when you're down in the gorge looking up at it.

A very rough, rocky, and steep descent follows. *Take great care. All fours are needed.* You descend under a thick canopy of vegetation, cool and dark. Dropping as far as you can *safely* go (**40min**), you still cannot reach the foot of the falls. You look through trees, to see the waterfall thunder down on to the rocks below, where three gushing arms of water cascade into a pool.

On your return climb, stop at the boulders, scramble under the largest one, and climb the rocky nodule behind it. From here you have another fine view over the gorge and falls. Eye-catching outcrops of granite with their incredible shapes turn the landscape into an exhibition of stone sculptures.

Then return to the snack bar La Cascada (**1h20min**).

25 BONIFACIO • CAPU PERTUSATO • BONIFACIO

Distance/time: 7.5km/4.5mi; 2h40min

Grade: easy; a walk for all the family. Can be very windy: on such days *do not* venture near the edge of the cliff!

Equipment: walking shoes, sunhat, sunglasses, suncream, cardigan, long trousers, long-sleeved shirt, swimwear, raingear, picnic, water

How to get there: 🚌 to Bonifacio (Timetable 19), *in season only*, or 🚗 rental car

To return: same bus or car

If you're anywhere near the south of Corsica, then Bonifacio is a must. This dramatically-sited, cliff-hanging town, with its centuries-old narrow streets is most impressive. The walk too, is well worth your time. Wandering along the windswept cliff-tops on this southernmost tip of the island, you're virtually blinded by the chalk-white limestone bluffs and the dazzling navy blue sea that they overhang.

Begin the walk at the church of St Erasme by the port. (In the Genoese era this was the fishermen's church, since they were forbidden entry into the town.) Climb the flight of steps to the old town. Tall, ancient buildings (with facelifts) line the steep pedestrian way. The imposing citadel walls rise high above you, on your right. Two minutes up, a magnificent view awaits you at Col de Roch. You look along the sheer curving coastline of brilliant white cliffs. Sardinia is the island of low hills you see stretching across to the southeast. The chapel here at the viewpoint marks the site of the death of the last victim of the Great Plague of 1528, which wiped out 60 per cent of the town's population.

To head out around the cliffs, climb the paved path that ascends to the left. You have a fine view back

View back to Bonifacio from the coastal path. The houses seem to grow straight up out of the limestone cliffs.

towards the strategically-sited town and over into the inlet sheltering the port. Once on the cliffs, hold onto your hats! The paving soon peters out and you're following a worn path of earth and stones. The surrounding peninsula is flat, but endless gulleys (many of them hidden from view) bite into it. Low wind-bent junipers and maquis shade the landscape in dark green hues. Far inland you can see the tail of the Montagne de Cagna.

In a little over **10min** pass the shell of a building near the cliffs. It's very tempting to peer over the very edge of the cliffs, but *this is exceedingly dangerous*, because there's often a big overhang that could easily crumble away. Also keep well back from the edge if it's windy. Supervise all children carefully. All the way along you overlook the wind- and sea-eroded coastline (**P**25).

At **25min** you meet the lighthouse road. Just beforehand the path is littered with shards of glass, so take care if you're wearing soft-soled shoes. Follow the road along to the right; then, minutes along, when it forks, head right for the Phare (lighthouse) de Pertusato. Minutes later you circle a small gulley that empties out into the sea. Strike off here on a path; it takes you down to the edge of the sea in eight minutes, onto smooth white tongues of limestone.

Back on the road, you ascend past batteries and, a

little further on, the maritime observation tower. Crossing a crest, you get a closer look at Sardinia, only twelve kilometres away. The Iles Lavezzi form the necklace of rocky islets between the two islands. The lighthouse sits alone on the point ahead. Below the crest and just past a track turning off left, find a path ascending through the hillside scrub. Follow it. Squeezing through the thorny maquis, you'll see a wealth of rosemary and red-berried *Lentiscus.* Should you venture upon herds of grazing goats out here, go quietly by them. Two minutes through the scrub you rejoin the road. Turn left and, after 40m/yds, bear right on a dirt track. Not far down the track take the path descending the left-hand wall of a small gulley that cuts down to the shore. A curious piece of coastline eaten away by wind and water awaits you. A monumental salient of limestone dominates the hilly waterfront.

Just under **1h20min** from Bonifacio you're at the water's edge. Here you discover a small sandy beach obscured by the rocky shoreline. The small islet of Ile St Antoine, adorned with a cross, hides behind the monumental rock. Climb the rock for another fine view of Bonifacio. A blowhole lies unnoticed to the right of the rock. Approach the edge with the utmost care, as it, too, is eaten away underneath. Pay particular attention when gale force winds batter the point here!

Return the same way (**2h40min**). You may want to visit the lighthouse, which lies a few minutes along the road to the right (currently, it is open to the public).

Looking back to the cliffs at the end of the walk, on an October evening ... before heading on to the port or old town for sustenance.

TRANSPORT TIMETABLES
for the walks and picnics in this book

1 AJACCIO — LA PARATA (Bus No 5) 🚐

Daily departures from '7' or '14' on the Ajaccio town plan, page 8; journey time 20min. (Note that from 1/7 to 31/8 services are more frequent than those shown here.)

departs Ajaccio 07.05, 08.05, 09.05, 10.05, 11.05, 12.05, 13.05, 14.05, 17.05, 18.05, 19.05
departs La Parata 07.30, 08.30, 09.30, 10.30, 11.30, 12.30, 13.30, 14.30, 17.30, 18.30, 19.30

2 AJACCIO — PORTO — OTA 🚐

Departures Monday to Saturday only from '6' on the Ajaccio town plan, page 8. (From 1/7 to 15/9 services are more frequent than shown below.)

Ajaccio	Listincone	Sagone	Cargèse	Piana	Porto	Ota
07.30	07.45	08.15	08.30	09.00	09.30	09.45
15.30*	15.45	16.30	16.50	17.40	18.00	18.30
Ota	Porto	Piana	Cargèse	Sagone	Listincone	Ajaccio
07.30	07.45	08.15	08.45	09.00	09.15	09.45
14.00*	14.15	15.00	15.30	15.50	16.30	16.45

*On Saturdays departs 12.30

3 AJACCIO — MARIGNANA 🚐

Departures Monday to Saturday only from '6' on the Ajaccio town plan, page 8.

Ajaccio	Listincone	Sagone	Vico	Evisa	Marignana
07.45	08.00	08.30	09.00	09.45	10.00
15.30	15.45	16.30	17.00	17.45	18.00
Marignana	Evisa	Vico	Sagone	Listincone	Ajaccio
06.30	06.45	07.30	07.50	08.20	08.35
10.00*	12.45*	13.30	13.50	14.20	14.35

*The 10.00 bus stops in Evisa for 2h30min, before departing again at 12.45

4 AJACCIO — SARTENE — PORTO-VECCHIO — BONIFACIO 🚐

Departures Monday to Saturday only from '6' on the Ajaccio town plan, page 8.

Ajaccio	Col St-Georges	Propriano	Sartène	Porto-Vecchio	Bonifacio
08.00	08.40	09.45	10.05	11.45	12.30
16.00	16.40	17.45	18.05	19.45	20.30
Bonifacio	Porto-Vecchio	Sartène	Propriano	Col St-Georges	Ajaccio
—	06.30	07.55	08.15	09.20	10.00
14.00	14.30	16.10	16.30	17.35	18.15

5 AJACCIO — ZONZA — PORTO-VECCHIO 🚐

*Departures Monday to Saturday only from '6' on the Ajaccio town plan, page 8. (Note: These are high season departures; outside July and August, services will be less frequent and there are **no** services to Bavella.)*

Ajaccio	Aullène	Zonza	Bavella	Zonza	Piscia di Gallo	Porto-Vecchio
16.00	17.25	17.55	18.05	18.15	18.40	19.10
Porto-Vecchio	Piscia di Gallo	Zonza	Bavella	Zonza	Aullène	Ajaccio
07.00	07.30	08.05	08.15	08.25	08.40	10.20

6 AJACCIO — MARE E SOLE (VERGHIA) 🚐

Daily departures from '6' on the Ajaccio town plan, page 8. (Note: These are high season departures; outside 1 July to 15 September, services will be less frequent.)

Ajaccio, depart	08.30	10.00	11.45	14.30	17.00	18.30
Porticcio	08.45	10.15	12.00	14.45	17.15	18.45
Cruciata turn-off	08.50	10.20	12.05	14.50	17.20	18.50
Mare e Sole (Verghia) arrive	08.55	10.25	12.10	14.55	17.25	18.55
Mare e Sole (Verghia) depart	07.30	09.00	10.35	13.45	15.00	17.30
Cruciata turn-off	07.35	09.05	10.40	13.55	15.05	17.35
Porticcio	07.40	09.10	10.45	13.55	15.10	17.40
Ajaccio, arrive	08.00	09.30	11.05	14.15	15.30	18.00

7 AJACCIO — CORTE — BASTIA 🚐

Departures Monday to Saturday only from '6' on the Ajaccio town plan, page 8

Ajaccio	Vizza-vona	Vivario	Venaco	Corte	Ponte Leccia	Bastia
07.45	08.40	08.55	09.05	09.30	09.55	10.45
15.00	15.55	16.10	16.20	16.45	17.10	18.00
Bastia	Ponte Leccia	Corte	Venaco	Vivario	Vizza-vona	Ajaccio
07.45	08.45	09.00	09.10	09.30	09.50	10.45
15.00	16.00	16.15	16.25	16.45	17.05	18.00

8 PORTO — CALVI 🚐

Departures Monday to Saturday from the Porto junction on the D81 and the Place Colombe in Calvi. Departures in high season only (15/5-15/10).

Porto	Serriera	Bocca a Croce	Col de Palmarella	Galéria turn-off	Bonifatu turn-off	Calvi
08.00	08.15	09.10	09.40	10.30	10.45	11.00
Calvi	Bonifatu turn-off	Galéria turn-off	Col de Palmarella	Bocca a Croce	Serriera	Porto
15.20	15.35	16.10	16.40	17.00	17.45	18.00

9 CALVI — BASTIA 🚐

Departures Monday to Saturday from '3' on the Calvi town plan, page 9

Calvi	Algajola	l'Ile-Rousse	Ponte Leccia	Bastia
06.45	07.05	07.20	07.55	09.00
Bastia	Ponte Leccia	L'Ile-Rousse	Algajola	Calvi
16.30	17.35	18.10	18.25	18.45

10 CALVI — CALENZANA 🚐

Departures Monday to Saturday, in July and August only, from '3' on the Calvi town plan, page 9. Journey time 20 minutes. **NB: Double-check these times in advance!**

departs Calvi 13.30 and 19.00; departs Calenzana 14.00 and 19.20

11 CALVI — GALERIA — GIROLATA ⛴

Daily departures in season from '15' on the Calvi town plan, page 9. Exact dates vary; check in advance. The daily service may be interrupted in bad weather. Only the 'Christophe Colombe' stops at Galéria.

departs Calvi 09.00, departs Galéria 10.15, arrives Girolata 12.00
departs Girolata 14.00, departs Galéria 15.30, arrives Calvi 17.00

12 CALVI — L'ILE-ROUSSE 🚂

Departures Monday to Saturday only from '2' on the Calvi town plan, page 9; 31/5-26/9 only. Many intermediate stops are made en route.

Calvi	Ondari	Alga-jola	l'Ile-Rousse	l'Ile-Rousse	Alga-jola	Ondari	Calvi
08.00	08.14	08.35	08.50	09.05	09.21	09.40	09.55
09.00	09.14	09.35	09.50	10.05	10.21	10.40	10.55
10.00	10.14	10.35	10.50	11.05	11.21	11.40	11.55
11.00	11.14	11.35	11.50	12.20	12.36	12.55	13.10
12.15	12.29	12.50	13.05	14.05	14.21	14.40	14.55
14.00	14.14	14.35	14.50	16.05	16.21	16.40	16.55
16.00	16.14	16.35	16.50	17.05	17.21	17.40	17.55
17.00	17.14	17.35	17.50	18.05	18.21	18.40	18.55
18.00	18.14	18.35	18.50	19.05	19.21	19.40	19.55

13 PORTO — GIROLATA 🚢

Daily sailings in July and August only (weather permitting)

departs Porto at 09.00 and 14.00; arrives Girolata 1h later
departs Girolata at 13.00 and 16.00; arrives Porto 1h later

14 BASTIA — LAVASINA — ERBALUNGA 🚌

Year-round departures from '6' on the Bastia town plan, page 10).

Monday to Friday: departs Bastia every 30 minutes from 07.30 to 12.00 and from 13.30 to 19.00.
Saturdays, Sundays and holidays: departs Bastia every hour from 08.00 to 12.00 and from 14.00 to 19.00
Return journeys: same frequency — last bus 18.30

15 BASTIA — ST-FLORENT 🚌

Departures from '5' on the Bastia town plan, page 10. Journey time 1h.

July, August: departs Bastia 10.30 daily and 17.30 Mon-Sat; departs St-Florent 07.00, 14.00 Mon-Sat
September to June: departs Bastia 11.00, 17.00 Mon-Sat; departs St-Florent 08.00, 18.00 Mon-Sat

16 BASTIA — MORSIGLIA 🚌

Departures Monday, Wednesday, Friday from '5' on the Bastia town plan, page 10; from 15 June to 15 September only. (Note: the bus only goes as far as Macinaggio on Mondays and Fridays; on Wednesdays only it goes to Centuri Port.)

Bastia	Mac-inaggio	Rogliano	Centuri-Port	Morsiglia
17.10	18.10	18.20	18.50	19.00

Morsiglia	Centuri-Port	Rogliano	Mac-inaggio	Bastia
13.00	13.10	13.30	13.40	14.40

17 CAP CORSE EXCURSION BUS 🚌

Daily departures from '6' on the Bastia town plan, page 10; from 1 July to 15 September only. The bus stops for 90min in Albo for lunch.

Bastia	Erbalunga	Mac-inaggio	Rogliano	Centuri-Port	Morsiglia
09.00	09.20	10.00	10.25	11.00	11.10
Pino	Albo (arr)	Albo (dep)	Nonza	St-Florent	Bastia
11.30	12.45	14.15	14.25	15.15	17.00

18 BASTIA — PORTO-VECCHIO 🚐

Departures Monday to Saturday from '15' on the Bastia town plan, page 1(

Bastia	Casamozza	Moriani	Cateraggio	Ghisonaccia	Solenzara	Porto-Vecchio
08.30	09.00	09.20	09.50	10.10	10.30	11.20
16.00	16.30	16.50	17.15	17.30	18.00	18.45

Porto-Vecchio	Solenzara	Ghisonaccia	Cateraggio	Moriani	Casamozza	Bastia
07.45	08.30	09.00	09.15	10.00	10.20	10.45
13.30	14.20	14.35	14.45	15.20	15.40	16.30

21 BASTIA — PONTE LECCIA — CALVI/BASTIA —

Daily departures from '4' on the town plan page 8 (Ajaccio), '2', on p

Bastia, departs	06.50		08.00	08.50	15.00
Casamozza	07.20		08.33	09.27	15.29
Ponte Leccia (arrival)	07.52		09.09	10.02	16.01
departs for Calvi				10.08	
l'Ile-Rousse				11.32	
Algajola				11.44	
Lumio				12.00	
Calvi (arrival)				12.08	
departure		06.50			
Lumio		06.59			
Algajola		07.15			
l'Ile Rousse		07.30			
Ponte Leccia		08.43			
departs for Ajaccio	07.54		09.15		16.03
Francardo	08.04		09.26		16.13
Corte	08.32		09.57		16.41
Venaco	08.48		10.15		16.57
Vivario	09.06		10.35		17.15
Vizzavona	09.26		10.58		17.36
Ajaccio (arrival)	10.30		12.07		18.40
Ajaccio, departs	06.25		08.00		14.35
Vizzavona	07.58		09.26		16.07
Vivario	08.18		09.45		16.27
Venaco	08.38		10.04		16.47
Corte	08.58		10.25		1707
Francardo	09.26		10.51		17.35
Ponte Leccia (arrival)	09.35		11.00		17.44
departure for Calvi				10.08	
l'Ile-Rousse				11.32	
Algajola				11.44	
Lumio				12.00	
Calvi (arrival)				12.08	
departure		06.50			
Lumio		06.59			
Algajola		07.15			
l'Ile-Rousse		07.30			
Ponte Leccia		08.43			
departure for Bastia	09.43	08.49	11.03		17.51
Casamozza	10.16	09.28	11.36		18.25
Bastia	10.45	09.57	12.05		18.55

9 PORTO-VECCHIO — BONIFACIO 🚐

Departures Monday to Saturday from outside the Trinitour Office, at the top of Rue Pasteur. Journey time 30 minutes.

Departs Porto Vecchio 08.00, 13.00, 15.00, 19.00
Departs Bonifacio 07.00, 12.30, 16.15, 19.00

20 PORTO-VECCHIO — BEACH SERVICES 🚐

Daily departures from outside the Trinitour Office, at the top of Rue Pasteur (15/6-15/9 only). Journey time 30 minutes.

To Palombaggia 10.00 and 17.30; returns 10.30, 18.00
To St Gulia 09.30, 12.00, 15.00, 19.00; returns 10.00, 12.30, 15.30, 19.30

PONTE LECCIA — AJACCIO 🚂

page 9 (Calvi) and '4' on plan page 10 (Bastia)

	16.10	17.00
	16.44	17.35
	17.18	18.12
		18.20
		19.42
		19.53
		20.09
		20.17
15.00		
15.09		
15.25		
15.40		
16.52		
	17.24	
	17.35	
	18.05	
	18.25	
	18.44	
	19.06	
	20.15	

NB: These services are valid from **31 May until 26 September**. A slightly restricted, but still adequate service, is effective from 27 September to 30 May. Obtain up-to-date timetables from the station nearest you. **Note that some of these trains may not run on Sundays and holidays! Check in advance!**

	16.05	
	17.35	
	17.53	
	18.13	
	18.34	
	19.00	
	19.09	
		18.20
		19.42
		19.53
		20.09
		20.17
15.00		
15.09		
15.25		
15.40		
16.52		
16.59	19.11	
17.35	19.43	
18.05	20.10	

Index

Only geographical names are included here. For other entries, see Contents, page 3. *Italic* page numbers indicate a map, **bold** numbers a photograph (either of these may be in addition to a text reference on the same page). 'TM' refers to the walking map on the reverse of the pull-out touring map. 'T' refers to *timetable numbers* (see pages 129-133).

A country code for walkers and motorists

The experienced rambler is used to following a 'country code', but the tourist out for a lark may unwittingly cause damage, harm animals, and even endanger his own life. Do heed this advice:

- **Do not light fires.** Stub out cigarettes with care.
- **Do not frighten animals.** The livestock you will encounter when touring and walking are not tame. By making loud noises or trying to touch or photograph them, you may cause them to run in fear and be hurt.
- **Walk quietly** through all farms, hamlets and villages, **leaving all gates just how you found them.**
- **Protect all wild and cultivated plants.** Don't try to pick wild flowers or uproot saplings. Obviously fruit and crops are someone's private property and should not be touched. *Never walk over cultivated land.*
- **Take all your litter away with you.**

The following points are especially directed to walkers, and cannot be stressed too strongly:

— **Do not take risks.** Do not attempt walks beyond your capacity and **never walk alone.** Four people make the best walking group: in case of injury, someone can stay with the injured person, while two go for help. Always tell a responsible person *exactly* where you are going and what time you plan to return: if your party is lost or one of your group is injured, rescue services would be notified that much more quickly.

— **At any time a walk may become unsafe** due to fire or storm damage, or the havoc caused by bulldozers. If the route is not as described in this book, and your way ahead is not secure, do *not* attempt to continue.

— **Strenuous walks** are unsuitable in high summer.

— **Mountain walks** are unsuitable in wet weather.

— **Do not overestimate your energy**: your speed will be determined by the slowest walker in the group.

— **Transport** at the end of the walk may be vital.

— **Proper shoes or boots** are a necessity.

— **Warm clothing** is needed in the mountains; even in summer, take something appropriate with you, in case you are delayed or injured.

— **Extra food and drink** should be taken on long walks.

— **Always take a sunhat**; cover arms and legs as well on sunny days.